I0797446

EXODUS & EXILE

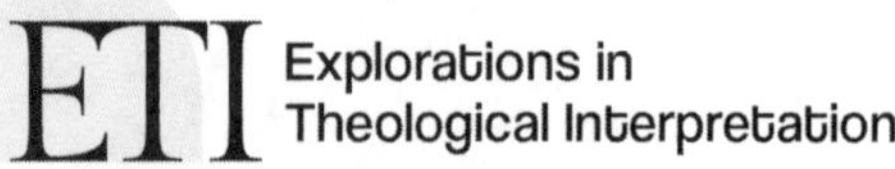

Darren Sarisky
General Editor

This series will consist of works undertaking and reflecting upon theological reading of the Bible. The current discussion of theological reading is one of the most generative and lively debates in contemporary theology. Theological reading, sometimes known simply as reading the Bible as Christian Scripture, does not refer to a single approach to bringing together biblical studies and Christian doctrine. It stands, rather, for a whole set of efforts to engage with the Bible so as to hear it speak today to theological questions that are alive especially within communities of faith. Though the vast majority of our volumes will read biblical passages in light of their ancient contexts, our books will have a decidedly theological-cum-hermeneutical focus, whether this comes from considering how the history of reception opens up new possibilities for interpretation; from retrieving traditional reading strategies, such as figural interpretation, that are broadly recognized as theological; from bringing interpretation into close relationship with ecclesial practices; or from working out the implications, for reading, of seeing the biblical text and its reader in a theological light. The series will publish well revised versions of the best recent doctoral work on theological reading and will also seek proposals from established scholars. The series builds upon the Journal of Theological Interpretation Supplement series, published by Eisenbrauns, an imprint of Penn State University Press.

EXODUS & EXILE

A Concise Biblical Theology

Karel Deurloo

Translated by David E. Orton

BAYLOR UNIVERSITY PRESS

Cover and book design by Elyxandra Encarnación
Cover art: The Mystic Mill, a capital in the basilica Sainte-Marie-Madeleine at Vézelay in Burgundy, France. Photo courtesy of Waldstein/Wikimedia.

The Library of Congress has cataloged this book under ISBN 978-1-4813-2330-7.
Library of Congress Control Number: 2024055886

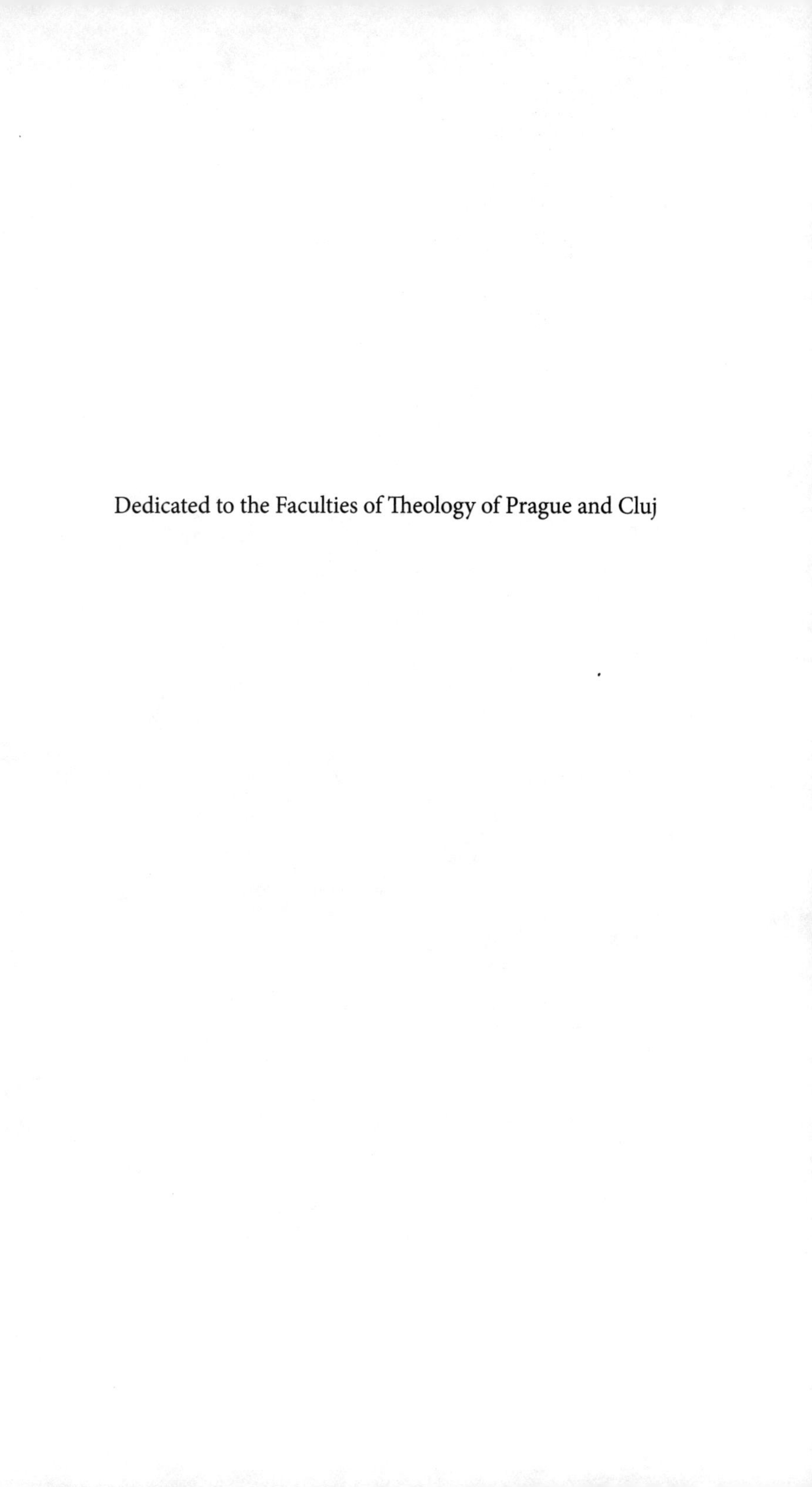

Dedicated to the Faculties of Theology of Prague and Cluj

Contents

Acknowledgments

Ten years ago, the idea arose to translate Karel Deurloo's "concise biblical theology" *Exodus and Exile* into English and to make it available to the English-speaking world, so that theologians and biblical scholars beyond the Dutch realm might benefit from Deurloo's insights. In the past ten years, many people contributed to make this happen. We would like to thank the translator, Dr. David E. Orton, for his dedicated work and for his willingness to discuss some translation choices at a later stage in the process. We furthermore thank Dr. Paul E. Koptak, professor emeritus of communication and biblical interpretation at North Park Theological Seminary, for his valuable advice during the translation process. We (Collin and Joep—and all readers of this volume) also owe immense thanks to Dr. Mirjam Elbers. It was she who first established contact between the Deurloo family and the translator. Then after that, six years ago (or so) Mirjam checked painstakingly over the entire first draft. She more recently introduced Collin to the project, and Joep to Collin, and both she and Collin went over the manuscript one last time at the very end.

Finally, we are most grateful to Mrs. Jettie Deurloo-Sluijter and her daughters, Janneke and Hermine Deurloo, who supported Karel's work during his life and have continued to lend support since his passing in 2019. Their moral and financial help were indispensable. Their dedication to the work of their late husband and father and their effort to promote it, also by creating the website www.kareldeurloo.com, has been encouraging and heartwarming. We gladly dedicate this volume to them.

Mirjam Elbers
Collin Cornell
Joep Dubbink

Introduction to Deurloo's *Exodus and Exile*

Collin Cornell and Joep Dubbink

What you hold in your hands is a "concise biblical theology," intended (as the preface says) "for a broad readership" (p. xxxiv). Indeed it achieved such a readership, and it was a near-classic work in its original Dutch context. Yet this description requires further explanation, since "biblical theology" is such a blurry and contested genre—let alone a *short* biblical theology written for wide circulation. The first section below describes just what this "short biblical theology" involves, and also what it promises to contribute to theological scholarship today. We highlight three areas:

- the *theological interpretation of Scripture*, which seeks to read the Bible as instruction for Christians, while taking seriously the insights of historical criticism;[1]
- a resurgent *dialectical theology*, which insists on God's otherness relative to natural human knowledge as well as various human projects;[2]

[1] The literature on theological interpretation is now vast; institutional organs include the *Journal of Theological Interpretation* (Eisenbrauns/ Penn State University Press), which also has a book series, JTSSup, several commentary series, and a range of consultations and sessions at the Society of Biblical Literature.

[2] See, for instance, the Society for Dialectical Theology, which launched in 2016.

- *postsupersessionist theology*, which rejects the longstanding error of Christian theology (called "supersessionism") according to which the Jewish people are no longer God's covenant partner.[3]

The final section of this introduction provides some biographical information about the book's author, the Dutch Old Testament scholar Karel Deurloo (1936–2019).

"Biblical theology" refers to a historically Christian and Protestant enterprise. On many definitions, biblical theology works across both Testaments of the Christian Bible. *Exodus and Exile* lives up to these expectations: it is Protestant and two testamental. Sometimes biblical theology is descriptive in purpose, aiming to articulate biblical conceptions of God (or relationship with God) only as artifacts of intellectual history. At other times, biblical theology is constructive in purpose: it aspires to make claims about who God really is, on the basis of biblical texts. *Exodus and Exile* falls very much under this latter, constructive charter.

But here it begins to diverge from other examples of biblical theology in the English-language world. Despite its concision, *Exodus and Exile* provides an overview of Hebrew Scripture's premier themes. In contrast to most biblical theologies, it does not seek comprehensiveness, trawling through the whole Christian canon and exegeting all its constituent parts. Instead it offers a tutorial for subsequent, individual acts of exegesis; see Deurloo's comment about biblical theology as "the necessary horizon of exegesis" (p. xxxiii). In this regard, it recollects its Reformed forebear, John Calvin's *Institutes*. The stated goal of that work was also preparatory: "to prepare and instruct candidates in sacred theology for the reading of the divine Word."[4] *Exodus and Exile* is as such a fitting textbook for prepastoral courses of study, a help

[3] As one example: the Society for Post-Supersessionist Theology. Its inaugural meeting happened at the 2018 Annual Meeting of the American Academy of Religion.

[4] John Calvin, *Institutes of the Christian Religion*, ed. J. T. McNeill, trans. F. L. Battles, 2 vols. (Philadelphia: Westminster, 1960), preface to the 1559 edition.

exactly to persons whose professional charge includes exegesis for the sake of preaching. We authors of this introduction have already assigned it, to good effect, in this connection.

Alongside its concision, *Exodus and Exile* differs from English-language biblical theology in the accessibility of its presentation. It does not seek an academic level of reference by sparring on all sides with other scholars. Occasional parenthetical names indicate the source of this or that phrase or idea, but the book's prose is readable, even homely. The project grew out of a longtime, well-practiced cycle of lectures, and it maintains the brevity and amiability of that context. This aural background is not incidental. As paragraphs below describe, the Bible translation by Martin Buber and Franz Rosenzweig was an important inspiration for *Exodus and Exile*, and one principal feature of that work is its attentiveness to the *aurality* of Hebrew Scripture.

Other Dutch Protestant theologians in the same lineage as *Exodus and Exile* demonstrate a comparable interest in the present-tense *hearing of the Word*. In fact, Deurloo's teacher, Frans Breukelman (1916–1993), was a legendary lecturer, almost a performer of Scripture. Theological students from Amsterdam would "make pilgrimage" out to his home in the Dutch countryside, where on weekends he would teach them with Hebrew Bible and Greek New Testament open on the kitchen table. Because of these students' urging and agitation, the theological faculty at the University of Amsterdam hired Breukelman into a brand-new position as associate professor of biblical theology.[5] This was one significant event in the creation of a so-called Amsterdam school of theology.[6] Deurloo himself did not approve the label, but he is nonetheless often classed as part of it, and *Exodus and Exile* showcases several common

5 Uwe F. W. Bauer, *All diese Worte: Impulse zur Schriftauslegung aus Amsterdam, expliziert an der Schilfmeererzählung in Exodus 13, 17–14, 31*, Europäische Hochschulschriften 23/Theologie Bd. 442 (Frankfurt am Main: Lang, 1991), 84.

6 The best introduction to the Amsterdam school in English is Martin Kessler, ed., *Voices from Amsterdam*, SemeiaSt (Atlanta: SBL, 1994).

features of the Amsterdam school—not least its indebtedness to oral performance, but more importantly its focus on the structure and keywords of the Hebrew text.

More materially, *Exodus and Exile* is distinct from other biblical theologies on offer in that it does not equally weight the two bodies of literature comprising the Christian Bible. It does not toggle between the Old and New Testaments, seeking to discern and synthesize their anthology of voices. In fact it criticizes this very framing. Instead of two, theologically coequal Testaments, *Exodus and Exile* engages Hebrew Scripture as Scripture per se and par excellence. The book does not defend this hermeneutical choice. Chapter 2 states merely: "What came to be known in the church as the 'Old Testament' is what the evangelists and apostles, the 'authors' of the 'New Testament,' called the scriptures or Scripture" (p. 15). The Hebrew Bible is quite simply "*the* prime authority" (p. 16), and within the Hebrew Bible, the five books of the Pentateuch are even more primary.

Exodus and Exile prefers the nomenclature of Law and Prophets, Torah and Neviim. These are the basic divisions of (Hebrew) Scripture. Over against this "dual core," *Exodus and Exile* calls the New Testament the "Apostolic Writings." These materials do not tender new theological content relative to Moses and the Prophets. Rather, following a quotation from Ben Hemelsoet, "the New Testament 'is' the Old Testament—read in such a way that Jesus is in the picture" (p. 16). In other words, *Exodus and Exile* goes about making its constructive claims about who God is on the basis of Hebrew Scripture, in particular the Torah and Prophets. It layers on quotations and insights from the Apostolic Writings as confirmation and specification.

Like some existing entries in biblical theology, *Exodus and Exile* responds to the task of identifying a center or "middle" of the Hebrew Bible. The book's author, Karel Deurloo, gestures toward this longstanding conversation: "Many biblical theologians have posed this question" (p. xxxiii). Deurloo agrees with one answer given in previous research: "YHWH is the God of

Israel, and Israel is the people of YHWH" (p. xxxiii).[7] Immediately, however, Deurloo interprets this claim according to the architecture of the Hebrew canon. The two major units of Scripture, Torah and Prophets, each center on a signature event that takes place between YHWH, the God of Israel, and Israel, the people of YHWH. As the preface already spells out, "Torah is concerned with the exodus and the Latter Prophets with the exile" (p. xxxiii). Notably—necessarily—for a "concise biblical theology" whose purpose is constructive, *Exodus and Exile* treats these signature episodes as theological disclosures. Exodus spells out YHWH's emancipatory power to set Israel free from enslavement. Exile spells out YHWH's mercy to restore fractured relationship with Israel. Together, these events set forth YHWH's character. They yield up the content of God's Name.

The rest of the book triangulates between these three foci: Name and Exodus and Exile. Chapter 1, "Exodus and Return," lays out the whole theological argument of the book in miniature, with a special focus on the divine Name. Chapter 2, "Law and Prophets," presents a different kind of bird's-eye view, not of the book but of the canonical organization of Hebrew Scripture into Torah, Former Prophets, and Latter Prophets. Chapter 3, "The Divine Name in Exodus," stages a theological reading of the Exodus within Torah. Chapter 4, "The Giving of the Torah and the Land," examines the closure of Torah and the start of the Former Prophets, wherein Israel inherits the promised Land. Chapter 5, "'I Will Lead You into Exile,'" theologically reads the Exile within the Latter Prophets. Chapter 6, "'He Cannot Deny Himself,'" exposits theological cross-references: moments when divine mercy to return Israel home appears already in the Torah, and when divine power to liberate through exodus appears within the Prophets. Chapter 7, "The Song of Praise and the Songs of

[7] See Rudolph Smend, *Die Mitte des Alten Testaments*, ThSt 101 (Zurich: EVZ-Verlag, 1970); also William McKane, "The Middle of the Old Testament," in *Covenant as Context: Essays in Honor of E.W. Nicholson*, ed. A.D.H. Mayes and R.B. Salters (Oxford: Oxford University Press, 2003), 261–83.

Ascent," turns to the Psalms to demonstrate the presence of both exodus and return in Israel's praise. The epilogue takes up and reprises the twin themes of exodus and exile—liberation and reconciliation—and draws these briefly into relation with the New Testament and with Christian systematic theology. It suggests the constructive potential of the book to other areas of theological discourse. It is to that promise we now turn, with an eye toward contemporary, English-language discussions.

Theological Interpretation of Scripture

A number of methodological commitments undergird *Exodus and Exile*, and they bring it within hailing range of several conversations in English-language theological scholarship. In common with initiatives to revitalize theological interpretation of Scripture, *Exodus and Exile* operates on the far side of modernity. Its interpretive outlook, that is, is postcritical. This is not a point the book makes at any length; only occasional asides show its acceptance of mainstream critical biblical scholarship. So, for example, concerning the exodus, chapter 6 begins: "The experience of emancipation took shape in Israel in the story of the exodus from Egypt. It is difficult to say when this happened. . . . *We may assume that the five books [of Torah] were given shape in the Second Temple period and for all sorts of reasons conclude that the story itself is not historical*" (p. 65, our italics). Or again, the same chapter allows that the golden calf story is a projection from "the history in the Land" back into the exodus story (p. 74), or that the author of Second Timothy is "Paul," in quotation marks (p. 75).

In spite of these occasional, modest acknowledgments of historical criticism, the overall emphasis of *Exodus and Exile* is on the *coherence* of Scripture's literary presentation. Critical biblical scholarship typically *differentiates*: source criticism picks out documents that formerly possessed their own literary integrity but were latterly pieced together into a new, composite document. Form criticism discerns even smaller units that circulated prior to their commitment to writing. By contrast with this differential procedure, *Exodus and Exile* reads the Pentateuch as a meaningful whole. The three books at the heart of Torah—Exodus, Leviticus, and Numbers—tell "the great story of the exodus, in which the commandments are given" (p. 18). But the first book, Genesis, already anticipates this signature Torah event. It narrates creation as a liberating act to provide humankind with a safe home in which to live, thus foreshadowing the major event of exodus. The rest of the book of Genesis focuses on the "firstbornship" of Israel. "Coming up out of Egypt" is an action of God's firstborn already in the first book of Torah, as Deurloo shows.

These exodus-anticipatory texts are, in the judgment of critical Pentateuchal research, late and redactional; they streamline otherwise hodgepodge materials. For *Exodus and Exile*, however, these editorial seams are interpretively crucial. Deurloo agrees with the Jewish thinker Franz Rosenzweig, who famously repurposed an abbreviation used in technical, source-critical scholarship. Source critics would tag certain biblical texts with an *R* to signify the final redactor (editor) of the Pentateuch. Rosenzweig on the other hand said: "we take this R to stand not for redactor but for *rabbenu* [our teacher]."[8]

Nearer to contemporary English-language theology, Deurloo's approach finds a parallel in the influential work of Brevard S. Childs. Like Deurloo, this biblical theologian also argued for the decisive importance of Scripture's final form—but not as a denial or circumvention of historical criticism. Rather, Childs observed that the long process of Scripture's development ended not by accident but as the result of theological discernment: the anonymous people who transmitted Scripture adjudged that in just this arrangement, these sacred traditions had reached a form best suited to their purpose of witnessing to God in any generation.[9] Childs's writings played a foundational role in making room for theological

[8] Franz Rosenzweig, "The Unity of the Bible: A Position Paper vis-à-vis Orthodoxy and Liberalism," in *Scripture and Translation*, ed. and trans. Lawrence Rosenwald with Everett Fox, Indiana Studies in Biblical Literature (Bloomington: Indiana University Press, 1994), 23.

[9] See, inter alia, Brevard S. Childs, *Biblical Theology of the Old and New Testaments: Theological Reflection on the Christian Bible* (Minneapolis:

interpretation of Scripture in the late twentieth century, and they continue to impact current discussion. *Exodus and Exile* floats free from Childs's detailed interactions with historical criticism; it does not, as he does, intellectually bid for canonical coherency. But ministers and teachers inspired by Childs's legacy will find in *Exodus and Exile* a partner and a proof of concept. Indeed the unassuming and unencumbered presentation of *Exodus and Exile* means it may feel less dated than Childs's work now does.

Another significant biblical-theological entry that bears comparison with Deurloo's "concise biblical theology" is Walter Brueggemann's *Theology of the Old Testament.*[10] Like Brueggemann, Deurloo attends closely to the form and language of Hebrew Scripture; both theologians alike focus pervasively on the profile of YHWH. They also emphasize God's inherence *within* the scriptural witness: when Deurloo asks, "Does 'God' exist?" his answer assumes the form of a recital; "[God] is there with his Name, he occurs as YHWH in Moses" (p. 32). This navigation of the "ontological" issue may resemble Brueggemann's own; he was, famously, accused of constructing a "paper God."[11] Unlike Deurloo, Brueggemann, however, rejects the pursuit of a "center" of Old Testament theology. Brueggemann's understanding of the relationship between the constituent parts of Hebrew Scripture is far more basically plural, even conflictual, and, unlike Deurloo, he draws in an organizational schema from outside of the Bible. Instead of Torah and Neviim, a courtroom metaphor, with testimony and countertestimony, structures Brueggemann's treatment of the Hebrew Bible. Brueggemann's interest in rhetoric far outpaces Deurloo's; the latter's observations remain more formalistic.

The scale of *Exodus and Exile* also sets it apart. Major books by Childs and Brueggemann are now several decades old; their

Fortress, 1992), 70–90; also Philip Sumpter, "The Trinity and the Canonical Process," *Theology Today* 72 (2016): 379–97.

10 Walter Brueggemann, *Theology of the Old Testament: Testimony, Dispute, Advocacy* (Minneapolis: Fortress, 1997).

11 For instance, Ellen Davis, review of *Old Testament Theology* by Walter Brueggemann, *Virginia Seminary Journal* (1999): 49–54.

successors in theological interpretation have been more modest. The ambition of *Exodus and Exile* to gather *all* the Torah under the heading of exodus, and *all* the Prophets under the heading of exile, is rare nowadays. A few English-language books construct a grand storyline for all of Scripture, and "big story of the Bible" approaches circulate widely at the popular level.[12] Yet here, too, *Exodus and Exile* diverges: the coherency that *Exodus and Exile* detects is not, in the end, *narrative*. Scripture does not amount to a single story. Nor is its unity principally *thematic*. At times *Exodus and Exile* uses the language of "theme," but it espies something more fundamental at stake in the events of exodus and exile. What scaffolds its vision of canonical coherency is *theological*, indeed *onomatological* (relating to names), and secondarily and relatedly, *linguistic*.

Here we arrive at the most distinctive contribution of *Exodus and Exile*. Expanding on Julius Wellhausen's summary statement that YHWH is the God of Israel and Israel the people of YHWH, Deurloo makes an effort to show how the Name YHWH is narrated in these two major events: exodus and return from exile. The four-lettered divine Name is the "one central point" (p. 1). Not that the four letters are holy in and of themselves (p. 30). Rather, they hold open space in the text (p. 6). They indicate, even in their opacity. The name theology of Deurloo's theological forebear K. H. Miskotte looms large here, and behind him, Rosenzweig.[13] But within English-language theological interpretation of Scripture, there is no comparable interest in the divine Name.

12 See, for example, R. Kendall Soulen's "standard canonical narrative" in his *The God of Israel and Christian Theology* (Minneapolis: Fortress, 1996); also Ellen F. Davis and Richard B. Hays, eds., *The Art of Reading Scripture* (Grand Rapids: Eerdmans, 2003); or again, Christopher J. H. Wright, *The Mission of God: Unlocking the Bible's Grand Narrative* (Downers Grove, IL: InterVarsity, 2006).

13 See K. H. Miskotte: "'Name' is, as it were, the A of the biblical ABCs." *Biblical ABCs: The Basics of Christian Resistance*, trans. Eleonora Hof and Collin Cornell (Lanham: Lexington Books/Fortress Academic, 2022), 17; also Barbara E. Galli, "Rosenzweig and the Name of God," *Modern Judaism* 14 (1994): 63–86.

Kendall Soulen's recent volume *Irrevocable* renders up the only possible exception.[14] Even so, for most readers, the claims of chapter 1 about "the four letters of the Name," the Tetragrammaton, will seem unfamiliar if not alien (p. 6). According to Deurloo, this is the exact intention of the biblical texts: confrontation with the unpronounceable Name of YHWH estranges readers from their general assumptions about "God" and directs their focus toward the special and particular witness of the texts themselves. Deurloo thus combines a dialectical insistence on divine *otherness* and divine *concreteness*—a paradoxical identity—with close reading of Hebrew Scripture. The problematic, misused word *God* needs redefinition according to the testimony of the Scriptures: only in the particularity of YHWH's liberating acts to Israel is its wider or more universal significance discoverable. In view of this proposal, *Exodus and Exile* stands ready to inform and resource the recent revival of interest among English-language theologians in *dialectical theology*.

Dialectical Theology

By focusing on the particular words and acts of YHWH, the Father of Jesus Christ, *Exodus and Exile* prescinds from the omni- prefixes of classical theology: omnipotent, omnipresent, omniscient (p. 2). These know too much in advance about God. They remove one from the concreteness of actual circumstance, from actual people one encounters. Since these divine omni-attributes stand equally behind all observable phenomena, they flatten attention to the particular phenomena that press in on human life. "According to Scripture," Deurloo writes, "everyday life consists of actions, encounters, conversations. This is where you have to find your way as you face the other person you have to deal with" (p. 12). This is also where God met Israel.

Once again, Franz Rosenzweig lies aback of this commitment to the everyday and the personal as the place where God makes the divine self known. "What do I know of 'all'!" he once

14 R. Kendall Soulen, *Irrevocable: The Name of God and the Unity of the Christian Bible* (Minneapolis: Fortress, 2022).

remarked. "What I have experienced and do experience is presence, power, knowledge, goodness—each in its and my hour."[15] But the conception of God in *Exodus and Exile* draws from a more proximate source. The "fundamental theological statement" that Deurloo commends comes directly from the Swiss Reformed theologian Karl Barth, though it is not cited as such: "The being of God is a being in action" (p. 11). God is *there* in God's actions, in YHWH's specific doings on behalf of Israel. Deurloo evokes the particular origin point of this knowledge of God with eloquence: "What is it that moves Israel? They don't really know how to describe it—they can only tell the story . . . We were slaves and were brought to the Land of freedom" (p. 12).

The Name and the deed hang together for *Exodus and Exile*: the particular referent and the concrete experience—these together are the basis of its constructive theologizing. As noted, the book identifies two primary experiences of Israel that the corpora of Torah and Prophets respectively orbit. Exodus and exile are not literary "themes." They are "concrete time-and-place" events that happened to Israel, that fill in the Name with a reservoir of meaning and memory (p. 13). "Anyone who wants to tell of the Name of YHWH must do so with the story of the saving exodus from Egypt and with the story of the experience of mercy in the return from exile" (p. 11).

The refusal of a generalized or generalizable approach to knowing God—truths read from anywhere off the face of the created world, claims that are always and in all places viable—is a hallmark of *dialectical theology*. Karl Barth was its originator; his *Römerbrief* was its manifesto. God's *otherness* is his notorious refrain. God is not identical with any created object, even with those created objects that God appoints to reveal God's self. In service of protecting the difference between God and not-God, Barth and his aftercomers leveraged the concept of *event*. Instead

15 Franz Rosenzweig, "A Note on Anthropomorphisms in Response to the *Encyclopedia Judaica*'s Article," in *God, Man, and the World: Lectures and Essays*, ed. and trans. Barbara E. Galli (Syracuse, NY: Syracuse University Press, 1998), 101.

of being in an ongoing or perennial or substantial way that would render God accessible on human terms, God acts, punctiliarly, indeed like a mathematical point, without extension. God is therefore unpossessable. One well-known *Römerbrief* quote sets out some of the basic coordinates of dialectical theology:

> The point on the line of intersection is no more extended onto the known plane than is the unknown plane of which it proclaims the existence. The effulgence, or, rather, the crater made at the percussion point of an exploding shell, the void by which the point on the line of intersection makes itself known in the concrete world of history, is not—even though it be named the Life of Jesus—that other world which touches our world in Him. In so far as our world is touched in Jesus by the other world, it ceases to be capable of direct observation as history, time, or thing.[16]

Barth and the other dialectical theologians of the early twentieth century oriented this theology of an uncapturable, event-ful God toward the cultural capture of God they observed in German society. In response to the fusion of God into the German colonial project or into the German war effort, they uttered a resounding *No*. Recent efforts to recover dialectical theology for the twenty-first century address a similar basic concern. Christianity in North America has fused with interrelated projects of nationalism, white supremacy, and heteropatriarchy. Exponents of dialectical theology envision it as a way of dissenting from this merger, of unpossessing God once more.

Exodus and Exile concurs that God's being is in act; God comes to humans punctiliarly. As such, it is a resource for present-day dialectical and dissident theologies. It is alert to the same ever-present possibilities of folding God into human projects—including the "toughness of the nation" and "the buoyancy of the economy" (p. 12). Instead of a christological crater where the other world of God touches ours, *Exodus and Exile* understands the divine Name YHWH as the "percussion point." In

16 Karl Barth, *The Epistle to the Romans*, trans. Edwyn C. Hoskyns (Oxford: Oxford University Press, 1933), 29.

concert with Barth, Deurloo holds that it is because God is faithful and constant that these past instances of intersection can raise our latter-day expectations for how God might act again here and now. "YHWH will not constantly be the same, but he will be the same person as then and there" (p. 13)—this is Deurloo's version of Barth's oft-quoted verse, "Jesus Christ is the same yesterday, today, and forever" (Heb 13:8).[17]

If this is the theological, even *onomatological*, touchpoint of *Exodus and Exile*, much the same dialectical reasoning informs its thoroughly *linguistic* interest. The whole volume is peppered with observations about Hebrew words and phrases. Chapter 1 lingers on the first line of the Ten Commandments: "I am YHWH-your-God who brought you out of the land of Egypt" (Exod 20:2). It suggests that the verb *bring* might better be translated "cause to move out." Without flagging it as such, this proposal conforms the English (and original Dutch) translation more closely to the Hebrew causative verb form (Hiphil)—and for Deurloo this stresses the active role that Israel, and in its wake the reader, should play in participating in their own emancipation. A later chapter posits: "*Moving out* is the primordial word for Israel" (p. 40), and biblical verses cited across the whole book italicize this catchphrase. It is just an example of how Deurloo finds meaning in reading the words and the texts closely.

The close engagement with the warp and woof of the Hebrew language in *Exodus and Exile* does not emerge from an antiquarian interest, nor from a fundamentalist conviction about the sacredness of the "original text." Rather, Deurloo's linguistic attentiveness dovetails with his dialectical vision. YHWH acted transformatively in such-and-such discrete moments of Israel's ancient life. But the communities that sustained these emancipatory and mercy-laden experiences treasured those memories; more than that, they held onto them and passed them along because they believed that YHWH "will be the same person [now]

[17] See George Hunsinger, "The Same Only Different: Karl Barth's Interpretation of Hebrews 13:8," in *Thy Word is Truth: Barth on Scripture*, ed. George Hunsinger (Grand Rapids: Eerdmans, 2012), 112–24.

as then and there." In that work of transmission, the medium of these key stories matters. *Speech*—that is to say, the spoken word, live, present-tense announcement—brings the stories of Yhwh much more directly into the ears and hearts of their listeners than the written page. What's more, the actual *forms* of biblical Hebrew preserve (and demand) that *spokenness*. By repeating and riffing on keywords and linked phrases, the scriptural text drums them into the present. By sequencing the text into short "breath units," Hebrew Bible passages summon their readers and reciters into a kind of performance. In Deurloo's words, "The concrete time-and-place connections of the stories and prophecies about them . . . have been written down so that they will have a *here-and-now* effect in liturgical reading, with a view to tomorrow and to anywhere" (p. 13).

Here again *Exodus and Exile* follows Franz Rosenzweig. He wrote in 1925 that books originally served the spoken word—but that writtenness, or scripturality (German: *Schrifttum*) had overtaken in the modern world. Books are no longer, as they were in antiquity, aides-mémoires for individual, out-loud readings. Rather, books are "dumb" and, "because dumb, detached from man, full of unlimited possibility, but therefore damned to exile in space and time."[18] Read in silence, they do not impinge on the present. They are timeless. However, Rosenzweig said about Scripture that "this book alone must not, even *qua* book, enter entirely into *Schrifttum*, into literature. Its unique content forbids it to become wholly *Schrift*. It must remain word."[19] Rosenzweig and his cotranslator Buber found that Scripture "escapes the specifying and distancing power of *Schrift*" exactly through its literary forms: its catchwords and wordplays, its patterns and segmentations. Consequently, even in translation, Scripture must not depart from these forms; the medium is integral to the message. A few Dutch Protestant thinkers before Deurloo took up this same commitment to the

18 Franz Rosenzweig, "Scripture and Word: On the New Bible Translation," in Rosenwald with Fox, *Scripture and Translation*, 40.

19 Rosenzweig, "Scripture and Word," 41.

forms of Hebrew Scripture, first K. H. Miskotte and then, more programmatically, Deurloo's teacher Frans Breukelman.

Postsupersessionist Theology

Exodus and Exile contributes to the theological interpretation of Scripture and to recent efforts at retrieving dialectical theology. It also deserves a place amid recent literature on post-supersessionist Christian theology. *Supersessionism* is a term designating the theological error that God's covenant relationship with the Jews is superseded, obviated, abrogated; often it includes a dynamic of *replacement*, according to which, after Christ, God's primary covenant relationship now pertains to the church and not to Israel. Many documents by the Roman Catholic Church as well as ecumenical Protestants have since World War II renounced this theological error and have reasserted the permanent status of Israel as God's people. To that tide of writings, *Exodus and Exile* adds a brief and worked-out biblical-theological example. Its onus is tutorial and preparatory, its goal constructive. It does not spend down its few sections and paragraphs defending Israel's primacy in God's economy. Nonetheless, this is everywhere its working assumption. The fact that it draws so heavily on the Jewish thinkers Rosenzweig and Buber evidences its receptiveness to the continuing spiritual validity and insight of Judaism. Its focus on the texture of Hebrew Scripture means that it works from a text shared in common with the synagogue, and hence a site of interreligious exchange and mutual openness. Finally, too, it does overtly, albeit briefly, compass the relation of church and Israel. After noting that this "concise biblical theology" follows the sequence of the Jewish canon, abbreviated TNK (Torah, Neviim, Ketuvim), Deurloo writes (p. 101):

> Despite that connection [of canonical sequence] with the synagogue, considerations remained within the time and space of the ecclesia, and not just because we [gentile Christians] always read the Apostolic Writings alongside them. No matter how much has to be learned there, the synagogue reads TNK differently. For the ecclesia, "the days of the Messiah"

> have dawned, in which *goyim*, baptized in the name of Jesus, read with the synagogue from this perspective.

He goes on:

> In the words of the letter to the Ephesians [baptized *goyim*], they may regard themselves as "fellow-citizens of the saints and members of the household of God" (2:19). As *fellow*-citizens—and only so—they may read the story of exodus and exile as their own as well, without for a moment losing sight of the fact that the words were spoken to Israel. They have a share in the blessing of Abraham. Israel, as the people of YHWH, remains for them the representative of humanity. A Jesus separated from Israel is no longer the Christ.

These brief comments are at once hermeneutical, addressing the scriptural reading practices of gentile Christians; christological, in that they frame the material theological difference underlying differing hermeneutical strategies of ecclesia and synagogue vis-à-vis Torah; and ecclesiological. They protect the priority of Israel as the people of YHWH and the original and ongoing addressees of God's word; they envision a joining through baptism of *goyim*—so that they may become secondary recipients of the word of YHWH and sharers in Abraham's blessing.

About the Author

Karel Adriaan Deurloo was born on January 25, 1936, in Amsterdam, the elder of two brothers. His father was a civil servant working for the tax authorities. The Deurloo family were originally farmers from Zeeland, the most southwestern province of the Netherlands. Deurloo was as proud of his provenance from Zeeland as his citizenship of Amsterdam.

During his years at the renowned Hervormd (Reformed) Lyceum in Amsterdam, it was his inspiring teacher of Dutch literature, Simon van Lienden, who made him enthusiastic about studying theology. At the theological faculty of the University of Amsterdam in the 1950s, he encountered a group of professors that had been newly formed in 1946, all enthusiastic teachers who knew how to inspire each other and their students. In addition to names such as J. N. Sevenster (New Testament), C. W. Mönnich (church history), and G. C. van Niftrik (systematic theology), Deurloo's later dissertation supervisor Martinus A. Beek (Old Testament) should especially be mentioned. Deurloo learned Hebrew from Aleida G. van Daalen, and he appreciated her approach to the Hebrew texts; their friendship and collaboration was lifelong.

Frans H. Breukelman was another key inspiration to Deurloo. Breukelman was a Dutch Reformed pastor who was inspired by Karl Barth and by K. H. Miskotte to supplement their theological approaches with a more in-depth exegesis of the biblical texts. Breukelman developed his own method and style of reading and interpreting Scripture, focused on structural and literary analysis, long before Robert Alter started pioneering in this field. As mentioned above, from around the 1950s, Breukelman gained a dedicated group of followers among theological students in Amsterdam. Their weekend pilgrimages to his home suggest that he was filling a gap in their regular theological curriculum—namely, how to read Scripture *coherently* and with an eye to their task of weekly preaching. Breukelman was appointed associate professor on the University of Amsterdam theological faculty in 1968, under students' pressure. While Deurloo's approach differs from Breukelman's, he always valued Breukelman's contributions; more than that, he considered him his chief teacher. In this respect alone, Deurloo stood apart, since many academic circles looked askance at Breukelman, a former pastor and frequent polemicist who never completed a PhD.[20]

The first years of Deurloo's professional career coincided with the 1960s, when as in secular history so also in biblical studies, scholars were searching for new roads beyond the historical criticism still prevalent in Old Testament studies at that time. After acquiring his PhD with a study of the story of Cain and Abel (Genesis 4) in 1967, Deurloo became a youth pastor in Eindhoven

[20] Nevertheless, more than thirty years after his death, two recent PhD theses have been devoted to his work, one by Gerard van Zanden (2019) and the other by Marco Visser (2022).

(1967) and later a student pastor in Amsterdam (1971). In 1975 he was appointed professor of Old Testament at the University of Amsterdam, succeeding his teacher and promoter Beek.

From the end of the 1960s, Deurloo made a name for himself as a leading exponent of what came to be known as the "Amsterdam school of exegesis." This movement generated both enthusiastic supporters and equally enthusiastic opponents. As a professor, Deurloo attracted masters-level students and PhD students from the Netherlands and soon also from abroad. The number of PhDs completed under his supervision is more than ten; the number of masters students doing a major or minor subject in Old Testament is difficult to assess but must be at least forty or fifty. A few PhD theses Deurloo supervised have been published in English.[21]

In the beginning, foreign students came mainly from Germany. They often experienced the Amsterdam approach to reading Scripture as a breath of fresh air in comparison to the German universities, where the *differential procedure* of historical criticism remained dominant (as it still does). Deurloo also attracted students from countries in Middle and Eastern Europe, especially from what was then Czechoslovakia. There were increasing contacts with Prague; Deurloo was one of the founders of the Colloquium Biblicum, an annual conference on the Bible and biblical theology that is still held today but has its roots in the time before the fall of the Iron Curtain in 1989. In those early days, the classes he taught were illegal, often held in student dormitories with one chair and two bunk beds full of students, and with only photocopies from the Hebrew Bible as texts. The Protestant Theological Faculty of Charles University in Prague recognized the importance of these contacts by awarding Deurloo the Jan Amos Comenius Medal (1994) and an honorary doctorate (2009). In 1995 he had already received an honorary doctorate from the Faculty of Protestant Theology and Religious Studies in Brussels.

[21] For example, Richtsje Abma, *Bonds of Love: Methodic Studies of Prophetic Texts with Marriage Imagery (Isaiah 50:1–3 and 54:1–10, Hosea 1–3, Jeremiah 2–3)*, Studia Semitica Neerlandica 40 (Assen: van Gorcum, 1999).

Over the course of his career, Deurloo wrote more than thirty books, a few of which have been translated into German, English, Czech, or Hungarian, and a multitude of articles. Only a small selection of these materials has been translated into English.[22] Deurloo intended many of his writings for a wider audience than only academic theological circles. He was driven to make the emancipatory message of the Bible known to ordinary people. Though often critical of developments in his church, he preached regularly and remained a loyal member of his local church community in Amsterdam.

In 1996, Deurloo was appointed professor of biblical theology at the seminary of the Dutch Reformed Church, affiliated with the University of Amsterdam. While this was generally regarded as a lower position than a full professorship at the state university level, Deurloo did not regard it as such: on the contrary, he was proud of being the only full-time teacher of biblical theology in the Netherlands, and his position inspired him to make the results of his exegetical work even more fruitful for theology, especially for ministers in training. It was in those days that he started the series of volumes called *Short Biblical Theology* that eventually included four volumes, of which *Exodus and Exile* is the first.[23] Deurloo occupied the biblical theology chair until his retirement in 2000.

Regrettably, Deurloo's professorship in biblical theology was discontinued after his retirement in 2000, and with that event, the study of theology effectively disappeared from the University of Amsterdam, leaving only a faculty of humanities with a department of religious studies. Deurloo was utterly disappointed; he

22 Martin Kessler edited two collections sampling from the Amsterdam school, including contributions by Deurloo: Kessler, *Voices from Amsterdam: A Modern Tradition of Reading Biblica Narrative* (Atlanta: Scholars, 1994), and Kessler, ed., *Reading the Book of Jeremiah: A Search for Coherence* (Winona Lake, IN: Eisenbrauns, 2004). See also Martin Kessler and Karel Deurloo, *A Commentary on Genesis: The Book of Beginnings* (New York: Paulist Press, 2004).

23 The other volumes are (titles translated): *King and Temple* (2004); *Our Lady Gives Birth to a Son* (2006); *Creation from Paul to Genesis* (2008).

regarded it as nothing less than disastrous for constructive theology based on the Bible. He nonetheless remained active in lecturing and writing. In 2003 he was appointed professor anew, again in biblical theology, but now at the Vrije Universiteit (Free University) in Amsterdam, in the endowed chair of the Dirk Monshouwer Foundation that he cofounded. In 2006, reaching the age of seventy, he voluntarily retired from this post, making room for younger theologians. I (Joep Dubbink) had the privilege to succeed him in that chair.

We would not do justice to Karel Deurloo if we only mentioned his professional career as a theologian, given that the richness of his life included so much more: he was the husband of his childhood sweetheart, the sculptor Jettie Deurloo-Sluijter, the father of two daughters, Janneke and Hermine, and a lover of classical music—a love he practiced both by listening and by making music on his self-built harpsichord. He enjoyed poetry and literature and explored intersections between Bible and culture. He wrote a good number of church hymns, six of which were included in the 2013 Dutch hymnal, and he authored several biblical "music plays" or operas. One of these, *Jonah the Naysayer*, set to avant-garde music by the Dutch Willem Breuker ensemble, was performed on many stages in the Netherlands and released on DVD (2005). Deurloo could also appreciate a good glass of wine and certainly a glass of dark beer in Prague's inner city, which he knew like the back of his hand. His students will remember him as an inspiring teacher, and his PhD students as a very involved and interested supervisor, who knew when to adjust and when to let go.

In 2010, Deurloo was struck by a massive cerebral infarction. Despite a long period of rehabilitation, almost complete aphasia remained, halting any further theological work. It was hard to see someone so verbally gifted become virtually unable to speak. He continued to receive regular visits from former colleagues and students, who read him stories and poetry and kept him informed as much as possible about their work. He passed away on June 1, 2019, after a short illness. His memorial service in the

Thomas Church in Amsterdam was attended by a large number of people, including many of his students.

Collin Cornell (1988) is Assistant Professor of Bible and Mission at Fuller Theological Seminary (USA).

Joep Dubbink (1958) is part-time Professor for Biblical Theology (Dirk Monshouwer Chair) at Vrije Universiteit, Amsterdam and a minister in the Protestant Church in the Netherlands.

Preface

For me, biblical theology was always the necessary horizon of exegesis. But how do you teach it as a subject? Frans Breukelman's book on key biblical terms, *Devarim*, is certainly an enduring support.[1] In this work he sketches a structure that lies behind the Bible's many theologies, such as the theology of the book of Genesis or the theology of Matthew's Gospel (the subject of some of his own writing). Within the great diversity of the biblical witness I wanted to point to something thematic that would at the same time cast light on the coherence within the collection of books. Is there a *center* to these many theologies—starting with the Hebrew Bible? Many biblical theologians have posed this question, and one of the answers they have given is the covenant formula: "YHWH is the God of Israel, and Israel is the people of YHWH." True though this may be, I wanted to nuance this somewhat and give it sharper contours. What is the "center" of the categories of the Old Testament canon: Torah, the Prophets, the Writings? By its nature the latter falls to some extent outside this question, but the Torah is concerned with the exodus and the Latter Prophets with the exile. The "center" of the Former Prophets

[1] Editors' note: Frans H. Breukelman, *Debharim: Der biblische Wirklichkeitsbegriff des Seins in der Tat* (Kampen: Kok, 1998).

is the figure of David, or to be more precise, king and temple. It seemed to me a simple and canonically given concept that provided a perspective from which the Apostolic Writings could subsequently be examined. Students, ordination candidates, and others attending various courses I have taught found it a helpful aid to reading, and audiences at guest lectures in Prague and Cluj responded similarly, asking, "Do you have this in writing?" Unusually for me, I made a promise to put it in writing. That was how this first short volume, a "concise biblical theology," came into being, intended for a broad readership. It will need to be followed up, because these pages say nothing, as yet, of the "center" of the books of Joshua to Kings.

Why not begin with the creation? Well yes, there are reasons for that, but a short volume on "creation from Paul to Genesis" is still to come. People asked more questions. It seems it will have to be a series, but I do not expect to be writing the following volumes on my own. This first volume is, however, a principled beginning.

A long reading list could be added, but this is not an academic book. I confine myself to the occasional mention of a name in parentheses to show that not all I write is from me. The translations of Bible quotations—in the Dutch edition—are a florilegium from a variety of Dutch Bible translations (in the English from the New Revised Standard Version), often adjusted to allow a particular Hebrew usage or certain connotations to become apparent. This is, I think, essential sometimes. For example, it is often not too important whether one *departs* from or *goes up* from Egypt, but in some cases it certainly is. I have quoted liberally but not sufficiently. I would like to see readers with a Bible to hand, as they would in a classroom. From time to time it may be, moreover, worth looking up Bible passages referred to.

What I think all this is mainly about is expressed in the epilogue.

Karel Deurloo

Translator's Note

For the English text, biblical quotations generally follow the NRSV. Where the author's own translation has a particular emphasis or turn of phrase not reflected in the NRSV, his wording is followed. An example is the use of the word *solidarity* (Dutch: *solidariteit*) in his translation of the Hebrew word *chesed*, which the NRSV translates variously with "loving-kindness," "steadfast love," "love," or "kindness."

For lines of Dutch poetry quoted in the original, the sense is given in prose. The poetic line divisions are observed, but no attempt has been made to create poetry in the translation.

David E. Orton

1
Exodus and Return

YHWH wins a people from the land of death and slavery: YHWH is "God." Motivated by mercy, YHWH grants his people a return from the land of exile: YHWH is "God." These are the two focal points in the Scriptures, which together also form the one central point: the Name YHWH. The entire content of the term *God* is provided by that Name. Whatever this term may mean before it is employed to say something definitive about YHWH, from this moment on *God* can only mean "the God of Israel," nothing else. So biblical theology can say nothing about God other than that. It can, like Israel, only speak against God or gods, "Not God or gods. No, YHWH is our God, and YHWH alone." The church can only reiterate what Israel says: "YHWH, the God of Israel, is God—for us too."

But wait a minute—isn't the church saying something different in the first line of the creed? "I believe in God, the Father, the Almighty, Creator of heaven and earth." A moderately well-educated citizen of the Roman Empire thinking in intellectual, monotheistic terms would have been able to recite these words without a problem. There is nothing specifically Christian or biblical about them. Creator? Certainly: *fabricator mundi*, "maker of the world." "Heaven and earth"? You could take this as a poetic expression for the cosmos with its visible and invisible aspects.

And "Father"? This term would only cause problems for this citizen of the empire when he heard the next part of the creed, which speaks of the Son in a very specific way. But Father, the Father or Mother of all—who could take issue with that? As a prefix, *all-* or *omni-* seems to be an automatic choice when speaking of God: almighty/omnipotent, all-present/omnipresent, all-knowing/omniscient, and for all time/eternal. Perhaps it is natural for human beings to speak about God in such general, all-embracing terms. Perhaps it is typical of paganism, which can be so impressively religious. But the Bible speaks, against the trend of these generalities, of the extremely special YHWH, the God of Israel. And what about God the Creator, of Genesis? This is the God that keeps the Sabbath.

When the word *father*—and very occasionally *mother* (e.g., Isa 66:13), as the Scriptures come from a male-dominated society—is sometimes applied to YHWH, then this word too is applied within the original sphere of that Name. The Name is expounded with stories, stories about the exodus from slavery and the return from exile. In Hosea 11:1 YHWH says of his people Israel, "Out of Egypt I called my son." There, in Egypt, is where it started. There Pharaoh says to Moses and Aaron: "YHWH? I don't know him!" And the natural consequence is, "And I will not let Israel go" (Exod 5:2). It sounds like the direct answer to the commission of Moses in the previous chapter: "You shall say to Pharaoh, 'Thus says the LORD: Israel is my firstborn son. I said to you, "Let my son go."'" (Exod 4:22–23).

In the book of Jeremiah we hear the same words in the context of the exile: "For I have become a father to Israel, and Ephraim is my firstborn" (Jer 31:9).

In the creed the term *father* is made specific in "Jesus Christ, his only-begotten Son." To take the creed from the perspective of biblical theology rather than church history, one has to point, first of all, to the beginning of the Gospel of Matthew, concerning the "genesis of Jesus Christ, the son of David, the son of Abraham" (Matt 1:1), that is, the messianic king who represents Israel. But what typifies Israel in the first place? "Out of Egypt I called my son" (Matt 2:15). The evangelist tells the story of the flight to Egypt so as to be able to quote the word of God from Hosea and apply it to Jesus. To speak biblically about "God" is to speak about the *father* of Israel, the *father* of the Messiah; and so the story of the exodus from Egypt needs to be told, and then the story of the later return from exile. As the God of Israel, YHWH takes pity on his children, like a father (Ps 103:13; Jer 31:2, 20). So for the apostle Paul he is "the Father of our Lord Jesus Christ, the Father of mercies" (2 Cor 1:3). When we address God in the words of the Lord's Prayer, the first request on everyone's lips, standing *with* Israel and on the authority of Jesus alone, is "Hallowed be your *Name*." YHWH is God. That is why stories have to be told; otherwise you can only say with Pharaoh, "YHWH? I don't know him."

1. ". . . Who Caused You to Move Out from Egypt"

The Ten Words, or Ten Commandments, tower architecturally above the liberal synagogue in south Amsterdam, like a banner above the space where the time from Sabbath to Sabbath is celebrated. Each year the whole of the Torah is heard, from Genesis to Moses's death in the last chapter of Deuteronomy. The heart of the matter lies in these Ten Words, spoken on Sinai, on the way "from Egypt, the house of slavery" to the Land, the *adama*, the ground where one can live, "which YHWH, your God, is giving you" (Exod 20:2, 12). The Ten Commandments have been called Israel's Magna Carta. They begin with a completely original "I," the one who addresses his people with the singular "you," "I and Thou" (in Martin Buber's phrase). "You" only becomes *you* when "I" speaks to you. But who is that Voice "at the mountain, out of the fire, the cloud, and the thick darkness" that "you" heard (Deut 5:22)? The answer to the question is given in the first introductory and crucial sentence of the Ten Commandments: "who brought you out of the land of Egypt, out of the house of slavery."

Shouldn't we have expected to read: "I am God, the Father, the Almighty"? Religious people of any persuasion would find that acceptable. But why should the Supreme Being, the sum of all divine power, have to turn to Israel in particular? That's a God you can believe in or—as is increasingly the case in our day—not believe in. It might be rather inappropriate to believe in this God. Just think of all the spiritual, social, and political effects it can have! Perhaps such a God has the attributes of Baal, whom Israel, too, got hung up on, according to Jeremiah (19:5), for example.

But why don't the Ten Commandments begin with "I am God, creator of heaven and earth"—perfectly good biblical terms, wholly in harmony with Genesis 1:1? No, it can't of course be "creator of the universe." In one fell swoop this would mean the loss of the specificity of the God of Israel. Anyone who prays the Lord's Prayer will know this. Just as his will is done in *heaven*, the hidden realm he has chosen as the place of his dominion (Pss 103:19; 115:16), may that will be done in the same way on *earth*, among human beings, in everyday life—his will, as heard in the Ten Commandments on Sinai. After all, that's what heaven and earth were created for; that's their purpose. They are not independent entities but must play their part in the history that is YHWH's concern. And only from that objective can the beginning of the creation according to Genesis 1:1 be understood. That is the precise reason why the Ten Words cannot have the heading, "I am God, creator of heaven and earth." In any case, that could be understood too generally, as something "one" says about "God": the maker of the world. Enlightened Greeks in Paul's day had no problem with this (Acts 17:15–34). But when the Psalms sing of the God who made heaven and earth, the turn of phrase is certainly related to this. Genesis 1:1 is the heading of the first overture of the first book of the Torah, which essentially deals with the birth of Israel amid the *goyim*, the peoples on earth (Breukelman).[1] This is the people that listens to the voice of YHWH-its-God on Sinai while it is en route from Egypt, the house of slavery, to the good land of freedom: he who set you on this path to freedom, he has thus become your God. That is how you got to know him, and in no other way.

1 Editors' note: Frans H. Breukelman, *Bijbelse Theologie I/2: Toledoth: de theologie van het boek Genesis* (Kampen: Kok, 1992).

At the head of the Ten Commandments we therefore read in both versions: "I am YHWH-your-God, who brought you out of the land of Egypt, out of the house of slavery" (Exod 20:2; Deut 5:6). Two comments are necessary in relation to the translation. *Bring* is the customary rendering, which is not incorrect. In the next chapter we shall argue that the translation *cause to move out* throws a stronger light on the exodus. Then the translation of the first words requires consideration. Wouldn't it be better to translate this as "I, YHWH, your God, who . . ."? What would be the difference? There may possibly be a third option: "It is I, YHWH, your God, who . . ." (a translation that might be reserved for when there is a participle). This translation is often rejected because YHWH would be subsumed into in his "act of liberation." But doesn't the customary translation sound like a "self-introduction formula"? "I am YHWH, your God . . ." Israel already knows that name, doesn't it? Isn't the focus primarily on the encounter with *God* that is *now* being experienced on Sinai? "I, YHWH, am your *God* . . ." One objection to this is that the Masoretes, the transmitters of the Hebrew text, did not read it this way. With the accents they have supplied they connect up "YHWH-your-God," and they do this more or less throughout the whole of the Bible. Is this just splitting hairs? Isn't it just a question of an accent? Yes, but that accent is not a triviality; it is of crucial importance. "*YHWH* is God" is saying something rather different from "YHWH is *God*." The introductory sentence to the Ten Commandments is not so much a "self-introductory formula" as it is a "presentation formula." "*YHWH* your God" presents himself *as* the one who caused you to move out of Egypt. Who he is emerges from that *deed*. Many texts could be cited in support. We shall confine ourselves to Exodus 6:6–7.

> I am YHWH,
> I will cause you to move out from the burdens of the Egyptians
> I will deliver you from slavery to them,
> I will redeem you. . . .
> I will take you as my people

I shall thus be God for you
and you shall know that I am YHWH-your-God
who has caused you to move out.

YHWH's "being-God" is not something separate from or added to his Name. It is contained squarely within that Name, in his deed. I, YHWH, will be God for you and only through the activity of that Name will you know what "being-God" means, in the exodus from Egypt. In that capacity, again and again YHWH will surprise his people with his presence. Who is Pharaoh, actually, when he says, "YHWH? I don't know him" and consistently, almost in the same breath, "I will not let Israel go"? Does he aim to make the divine Name impossible?

The four letters of the Name—the "tetragrammaton"—are rendered in English as YHWH, and are not to be pronounced, as in the Hebrew text (the *ketib*). In Hebrew the tetragrammaton is usually read (the *qere perpetuum*) as Adonai, "My Lord," or "the Name." The abbreviated form YaH is sung in the Psalms, for instance in "Hallelujah" (cf. Ps 118:5, 14, 18, 19), or it is said with Yahu or Yeho in theophoric names: Yesha-yahu (Isaiah), Yehoshua (Joshua). In the Greek version the ancient Hebrew tetragrammaton used to be written, but it was read (*qere*) as *kyrios*, "Lord." And so the Name remains an open space in the text, so holy, so uniquely "special," that a reading can only be a reference to the Name. What should our *qere* be? Most English versions are clear about this, writing LORD in capital letters, in accordance with Hebrew and Greek tradition. The Dutch *Statenvertaling* translators did the same with HEERE (Lord). German Jews borrowed the term *l'Éternel*, "the Eternal," from Huguenot refugees. Should we go back to the old Calvinist tradition? The problem with "the Eternal" is the connotation of a certain quality—more philosophical than biblical. Another proposal—"the One who is There" (Dutch: *de Aanwezige*)—misses the surprising thing that in the explanation of the Name in Exodus 3:14 we find the expression "I am who I am." That also applies to the Name *in* the biblical text. With the reading "the Present One" (Dutch: *de Tegenwoordige*) readers still don't entirely grasp the Name, but as they read they can get involved in the events being narrated. YHWH comes over you, by setting you on the path of departure, and that is at the same time the pathway of his commandments (Ps 119). Having been brought out of the house of slavery, or *service* in Egypt, you know YHWH by entering into the freedom of service to him as you *do* his commandments and thus also properly *hear* (obey) them: "We will do it, hear it" (Exod 24:7). And all Bible knowledge can only mean anything if it is in the service of "knowing"—with heart and soul, in word and deed—YHWH, "who caused you to move out." That fundamental clause rings out time and again, not only in the Torah but also in the Prophets. You can only speak of Israel's God by in the *first* place telling the story of exodus. In general this never happens, and in the church, unfortunately, only rarely.

True storytelling cannot be done without involvement. Caught up in the motion of the story, you also learn to understand the commandments as signposts along the way: the Torah as instruction. You might say that the *halakhah*, the rules for your conduct and life's walk, is set in the context of the *aggada*, the storytelling of the path through history that YHWH has traveled with you from Egypt to Canaan. That's what his Name stands for. The sanctification laws in the book of Leviticus are "signed" with that Name. In full: "I am YHWH your God, who caused you to move out from the land of Egypt, to give you the Land of Canaan" (Lev 25:38), or more concisely: "I am YHWH your God" (e.g., Lev 19:4), but "I am YHWH" (Lev 19:12) can also suffice.

The Name cannot yet be spoken of like this in Genesis, as the exodus still lies in the distant future, even if it is announced to Abram (Gen 15:13–16). In the introduction to this announcement, however, YHWH does speak the words of self-presentation: "I am YHWH, who caused you to move out from Ur of the Chaldeans, to give you this land to possess." In wording this, the storyteller was thinking of a text like the one from Leviticus quoted above. YHWH's being-God is locked into the deed of his Name. An anonymous prophet who sets the call of Gideon in an appropriate framework begins as follows: "Thus says YHWH, the God of

Israel: I caused you to go up from Egypt, I caused you to move out from the house of slavery. . . . I am YHWH, your God. Do not fear the gods of the Amorites" (Judg 6:8–10). This is your God, and no other (cf. Isa 45:5). The Torah story has to be told first so as to put the central theme of the Prophets in the right perspective.

2. "Merciful and Gracious . . ."

YHWH is God. Resounding in Moses's ears when he hears the voice of the Name call for the second time—after Exodus 3:14—are the words "YHWH, YHWH, a God merciful and gracious, slow to anger, and abounding in steadfast love and faithfulness" (Exod 34:6). What story is required in the *second* place in order "to tell the Name" (Ps 22:22)? The story of his mercy.

In the first chapter of his Gospel, Luke has Mary sing very appropriately: "Holy is his *Name* and his mercy is for those who fear him from generation to generation" (Luke 1:49–50; cf. Ps 103:13, "as a father . . ."). And her song of praise also concludes, "in remembrance of his mercy" (1:54). Zechariah borrows the word: "He has shown the mercy promised to our ancestors" (1:72). At the end of his song of praise we hear from his lips that the child John will prepare the way as a prophet "to give knowledge of salvation to his people by the forgiveness of their sins by the *inner* [NRSV: tender] mercy of our God" (1:77–78). The verb "have mercy, have pity" is sometimes also used in reference to people, but the answer to the question "Who is God?" has to be "merciful and gracious is YHWH, slow to anger, and abounding in steadfast love" (Exod 34:6; Ps 103:8). This saying occurs seven times in Scripture, usually beginning with "gracious and merciful" (Joel 2:13; Jonah 4:2; Pss 86:15; 145:8; Neh 9:17). Is this a generally applicable answer, or do you have to ask a specific question here too: When is he—or was he—merciful? Is YHWH always and in all places and before anyone else the Merciful One, or is he the Merciful One in the same way he is the Deliverer, namely from *Egypt* onward (cf. Hos 13:4)? Luke adds an aspect to the "inner mercy": "by the forgiveness of their sins" (1:77).

Let's take a look at the chapter in which the words *merciful* and *mercy* occur most frequently (6×)—the prayer of repentance in Nehemiah 9. In that prayer we hear the whole biblical history, starting with the creation (Neh 9:6). The phrase "Gracious and merciful . . . ," which occurs seven times in the Scriptures, resounds as an introduction to the episode of the sin associated with the golden calf (cf. Exod 34:6). Despite that episode, YHWH in his "*great mercy* did not forsake them in the wilderness" (Neh 9:17–19). When the people did not obey the "Law and Prophets" in the Land, YHWH gave them into the hands of their opponents. But every time Israel called to YHWH, he freed them in accordance with his *great mercies* (Neh 9:27). However, everything is pointing to that one time when the word "mercy" (Hebrew: *chesed*) really comes into its own, the moment when nothing else could be expected, the *exile*: "Then you handed them over to the peoples of the lands." But the very fact that they have returned to the Land and are now praying, is the sign par excellence of God's mercy: "In your *great mercies* you did not make an end of them or forsake them, for you are a gracious and merciful God" (Neh 9:31).

Many biblical texts look back to the Babylonian exile, but only with the realization that it is a miracle this backward look is possible at all. Having returned to the Land, Israel seems able to remember the exile as a bitter episode in which it had to repent (Isa 40:1), a period Jeremiah refers to as the "seventy years" (Jer 25:11; 29:10; 2 Chr 36:21). True, it has been an interval like this, but it should not be forgotten for a moment that the very occurrence of the exile deflected the impending threat of an absolute end. In his parable of the linen loincloth, Jeremiah left no room for doubt about this. Barely had he bought the loincloth when he had to hide the new acquisition, worn around his waist, in a cleft in the rock in "Perat." After many days he was allowed to go and recover it, "but now the loincloth was *ruined*, it was good for nothing" (Jer 13:7).

What is the location of "Perat"? In Hebrew it is the same name as Euphrates, the river that defines the land of exile. The explanation of the parable is, then, that YHWH has lovingly wrapped his *people* around his loins like a loincloth, wearing it as an adornment. But as it no longer listened to him, it was no longer any good to him: "It shall be like this loincloth, which is good for nothing" (Jer 13:10). Immediately after this comes a sort of tavern scene in which people raise filled wine jars one after another. As such jars, YHWH will dash fathers and sons against each other: "I will not pity or spare or have compassion so that I should *not ruin* them" (Jer 13:14). The effect of this is depicted right away: "The towns of the South are shut up with no one to open them; all Judah is taken into exile, wholly taken into exile" (Jer 13:19). The debt of the people is definitively irredeemable, as they have canceled the relationship with YHWH: "You have rejected me, says YHWH, you are going backwards. Now I am stretching out my hand against you and *ruining* you—I am weary of relenting" (Jer 15:6).

No matter how sharply the definitive end may be put into words, in the very same book of Jeremiah the moment of return arrives as a complete surprise. Certainly, this means a return from exile to the Land, but first and foremost it is an about-turn on the part of YHWH himself. Unexpectedly and inconceivably, something stirs in his being for which there is no reason or justification. It emerges completely originally out of who he is, from who he wants to be, true to his Name. Forsaken by his people, he seems unable to abandon his people to its demise. It is his Name—YHWH, I will be there, with you and for you—that he cannot deny. He wishes simply to be the God of Israel. He, the Merciful One, does what he is and says what he does: "I will restore their fortunes, and will have mercy on them" (Jer 33:26). It seems that YHWH is capable of this and of accomplishing it. It is in this that he reveals his power.

The church's confession of "the Almighty" in the creed comes immediately after "I believe in God the Father." It needs to be understood in accordance with Israel's Scriptures! In the book of Jeremiah too, YHWH looks upon his people "Ephraim" as a father upon his son. He cannot help but remember him in that fatal calamity of his own making: "Therefore I am deeply moved for him; I will surely have mercy on him" (Jer 31:20; cf. 31:9). He will succeed in making this people his own once again and in being the God of "Israel." If the term *almighty*—not a typically biblical word—is to be used, then it needs to be understood in reference to the almightiness of his mercy, which occurs in the return from exile. That is why Ezekiel compares the return with a resurrection from the dead (Ezek 37).

YHWH is the God who leads out of Egypt. In the continuation of this, equally, we read: "I am YHWH, your God, who teaches you for your own good, who leads in the way you should go [out of Babylon]" (Isa 48:17). You have been led out of slavery by your exodus from the land of death, Egypt. That is the first thing that is said by God in the Torah. In the Prophets we read the second thing, equivalent to it: You have experienced mercy in your return from exile in Babylon, where you had ended up after breaking your relationship with YHWH.

With this we have the two focal points in Scripture. Anyone who wants to tell of the Name of YHWH must do so with the story of the saving exodus from Egypt and with the story of the experience of mercy in the return from exile. YHWH is the only one deserving of the epithet, the ornamental title "God" because he is *there* in these deeds, concretely, directly, in the encounter with his people. His ineffable Name speaks in these stories—relating history.

3. Always and in All Places?

"The being of God is a being in action."[2] That is a fundamental theological statement. "God" is not a supreme being overarching everything and everyone in his eternity—a deepest or highest secret of the universe that you can feel, presume or imagine behind all phenomena. If "God" is there in his actions, then you have to deal with him, and then you have to ask: When and where? The answer "Over and over again!" can tend towards *al*ways and in *all* places. It's that little religious word *all* again. It takes all the concreteness out of the question of "God," unless of

[2] Editors' note: Karl Barth, *Church Dogmatics II.1: The Doctrine of God*, ed. G. W. Bromiley and T. H. Torrance, trans. T. H. L. Parker, W. B. Johnson, et al. (Edinburgh: T&T Clark, 1957), 262.

course you find him in yourself. Then he is simply the mystery of your own being, as long as you exist, but in that case "acts of God" are merely impulses from your self. You then need to be in conversation with yourself to find your way, and you may wonder whether that isn't more of a lonely adventure than a shared one.

Such thoughts do not arise in Israel. According to Scripture, everyday life consists of actions, encounters, conversations. This is where you have to find your way as you face the other person you have to deal with. You need to love your neighbor because he or she is just like you. The strange and crucial encounter that Israel experienced, however, is one with an entity that is entirely *other*. God? Surely not in the sense of the truly impressive mystery of the productivity of the earth, the power of female-male "erotic" procreation; not the toughness of the nation you are part of, which, using force if necessary, is able to deal with other nations or strengthen itself against them; not the vitality of healthy, powerful living; not the buoyancy of the economy and not even the creativity of word, sound, and image, which can amaze and move us so deeply. In short, not the world and its mysteries, nor the mystery behind the world, which remains eternally hidden.

So then, what is it that moves Israel? They don't really know how to describe it—they can only tell the story: It took us by surprise. We were slaves and were brought to the Land of freedom. That emancipation, that's what it was! That's how we came to be here at all. It affected us personally, in more than one sense. That was it—that's him. Not so much *that*, but *this person* can have a *name*. Or better: that's how we could tell who has a *name* and what freedom in his name means, and what it requires of us.

But Israel needs to say more than this. We used the freedom for ourselves, at the expense of people who needed us. We stood speechless at the forces of productivity. We grasped our opportunities for self-development. We forgot that someone who is liberated must also live a liberating life. We forgot the Name by which we are here and can only be here. We forgot that *this* God asks for love because he is human and takes humanity's part—for *us*. The Land that was given to us, liberated slaves, refused to play along and "vomited us out" (Lev 18:28) because *this* God, the giver, saw himself abandoned.

How can Israel tell this story? Because in the middle of his—apparently failed—adventure with Israel, YHWH proved himself to be truly God by achieving with his people, at that fatal lowest point, the turn to life itself. Then and there: "God" in Egypt and in Babylon—not just in the first instance but also in the crucial second, the God of Israel. That's what makes him *other* than all the gods, processes, and powers.

Isn't there more to be told? A great deal more *is* told, prophesied, and sung by Israel, but at its core the concern is with these two focal points: the Deliverer and the Reconciler, *then and there*. The concrete time-and-place connections of the stories and prophecies about them, however, have been written down so that they will have a *here-and-now* effect in liturgical reading, with a view to tomorrow and to anywhere. YHWH will not constantly be the same, but he will be the same person as then and there, for Israel and for the whole of humanity, represented in Israel, always and in all places. The particular story of Israel lays claim to being universal in its specificity. That's why on the day after the Sabbath the church listens with Israel to *this* narrated history, to this "fantastic story" (Dick Boer).

4. Beggar and Sinner

"What was the sermon about?" It's an old Protestant joke I remember from my childhood. You could always say, "About sin"—because that's what it was always about! People were reminded that they were sinners, possibly *converted sinners*. That's not how it happens in Scripture. One example: "You shall love the alien as yourself, for you were aliens in the land of Egypt; I am YHWH, your God!" (Lev 19:34). The commandment can also be used to interpret the other one: "You shall love your neighbor as yourself" (Lev 19:18). Your neighbor is easy to recognize: it's someone just like you. In the commandment about the alien you were reminded that you were an alien, that you are a *liberated slave*. Noordmans has pointed out that in the Gospel of Luke the parable of the rich man and Lazarus (Luke 16:19–31) comes before the parable of the Pharisee and the publican (Luke 18:9–14), and that the petition for one's daily bread in the Lord's Prayer comes *before* the prayer for forgiveness of one's debts.[3] Luke is thus following the scriptural order. Thus Mary's song of praise concludes *first* with the liberation from oppressive powers (like Pharaoh) and the giving of bread (as in the wilderness): "He has brought down the powerful from their thrones . . . he has filled the hungry with good things" *and then*, "He has helped his servant Israel, in remembrance of his mercy" (Luke 1:52–54).

[3] Editors' note: Oepke Noordmans (1871–1956).

2
Law and Prophets

What came to be known in the church as the "Old Testament" is what the evangelists and apostles, the authors of the "New Testament," called the Scriptures or Scripture. A few passages to illustrate this: "Have you never read in the Scriptures . . . ?" (Matt 21:42). "You search the Scriptures" (John 5:39; in John again in the singular, cf. 2:22). Paul went to the synagogue, as was his custom, "and on three Sabbath days argued with them from the Scriptures" (Acts 17:2). "Christ died for our sins in accordance with the Scriptures" (1 Cor 15:3).

In addition, we encounter the phrase *Law and Prophets.* A notable example is found at the beginning of the Sermon on the Mount. After the Beatitudes and calling the disciples "salt of the earth" and "light of the world," Jesus says: "Do not think that I have come to abolish the law or the prophets" (Matt 5:17). One might also translate this as "demolish," as if the Scriptures form a building he is going into to fill, to "fulfill." At the beginning of the Gospel of John it is said no less emphatically: "We have found him about whom Moses in the law and also the prophets wrote" (John 1:45). At the end of the book of Acts, Luke tells us that Paul speaks in Rome about the kingdom of God and about Jesus "from the law of Moses and from the prophets" (Acts 28:23). In his letter to the Romans the same apostle writes: "The righteousness of

God has been disclosed, and is attested by the law and the prophets" (Rom 3:21). For the authors of the New Testament, the Scriptures, the Law and the Prophets, are *the* prime authority, when they write their words about Jesus. The term *Old Testament* has become established, but for a reader of the New Testament it can only sound like the "good old" Testament.

Why should we prefer the phrase *Moses and the Prophets*? Because this is more characteristic of the collection of Scriptures: the Torah, the teaching of Moses; and the Neviim, the "Former Prophets" ("former" because they come earlier in the canon) and the "Latter Prophets" (the great trio Isaiah, Jeremiah, and Ezekiel and the Book of the Twelve Prophets). There is a single mention in the Apostolic Writings of a third category: the Psalms (Luke 24:44). These constitute the first book in the series that in the later Jewish canon is called the Writings, the Ketuvim (cf. the prologue in the deuterocanonical book Sirach). Hence the acronym TNK (Tenakh or Tanakh). Most of these Writings are in fact cited by the New Testament authors: Psalms, Job, Proverbs, the Five Scrolls, Daniel, Ezra, Nehemiah, Chronicles. They belong to the Writings, but still there is constant talk of Torah and Neviim. It is the dual core of what the Scriptures proclaim.

1. "They Have Moses and the Prophets . . ."

Already in his first chapter—in particular in the songs of praise by Mary and Zechariah—Luke leaves no possible doubt that for him the Scriptures are the starting point. So it is not at all surprising that he ultimately brings everything back to the Scriptures. The hearts of the disciples on the road to Emmaus were glowing at the Stranger's words: "Then *beginning* with Moses and all the prophets, he interpreted to them the things about himself in *all* the Scriptures" (Luke 24:27). Not a single text is cited, which is a good thing. Hemelsoet used to comment, "What is the New Testament? The New Testament 'is' the Old Testament—read in such a way that Jesus is in the picture."[1] In that case, the question "Who is Jesus?" cannot be answered by "Just read the New Testament!"

1 Editors' note: Bernardus (Ben) Paulus Marie Hemelsoet (1929–1999).

That is to rush things and—worse still—get things wrong. The answer has to be, "*Begin* by reading Moses and the Prophets."

Luke relates a parable about this, which he places significantly in the context of the brokenness of the world, the contrast between rich and poor (Luke 16:19–31). Despite this, humor sparkles through the story, as is often the case. He places grotesque images on Jesus's lips: when Lazarus (Eleazar, "God-is-help"—the poor man has no other help) dies, who is going to bury him? But just look, then there are angels and they carry him away . . . to heaven? No, to "Abraham's bosom," because he is sitting at the great banquet with Isaac and Jacob and all the prophets (Luke 13:28). Lazarus is given a place of honor: he is leaning against Abraham's bosom. The story is, however, directed to the rich man, who is not granted a name. Hearers of the parable may possibly recognize themselves in him. When he dies, he is of course given a splendid funeral. Then he opens his eyes in the realm of the dead, and what does he see? Lazarus with Abraham. But he's a son of Abraham too, isn't he? He calls out: "Father Abraham!" The roles seem to have been switched. He notices that he is now on the same level as "the beggar" Lazarus. He has to beg. Not, like Lazarus when he was alive, for a crumb of bread from the table but for a drop of water. Can't Lazarus dip his finger in water and cool his tongue in the flames where he finds himself? "Child," says Abraham touchingly, "remember your life"—and this should not go unnoticed by those listening to the story—"you have now changed places. Besides, we can't reach each other, the chasm between us is far too deep."

Child! That sounds a bit fatherly, doesn't it, coming from Abraham's lips? Will it touch a soft spot? The rich man continues: "Then, *father*, I beg you to send him to *my father's* house, for I have five brothers"—in line with the number of the scrolls of the Torah. Do the brothers need to be warned? But that would be completely superfluous. Abraham gives the only appropriate answer: they have Moses and the Prophets; they should listen to them. "Hear, O Israel!"

The rich man then comes with a kind of pseudo–New Testament punch line: "No, father Abraham; but if someone goes to them from the dead, they will repent." Abraham's reaction couldn't have been any sharper, and the Christian community has to take it as addressed to them too: "If they do not listen to Moses and the Prophets, neither will they be convinced even if someone *rises from the dead*."

The Messiah rose again "in accordance with the Scriptures!" (1 Cor 15:3). The Scriptures were the pro-gram, the pre-scription. Luke relates of the Risen One: "And he began with Moses and all the prophets . . ."

2. Torah: Exodus

The three middle books of the Teaching of Moses describe the movement out of Egypt, through the wilderness to the threshold of Canaan: "These are the names of the sons of Israel who came to *Egypt*" (Exod 1:1). At the end we read how the last commandments are given to the children of Israel "in the plains of Moab *by the Jordan* at Jericho" (Num 36:13). This exodus movement colors everything in the three books, Exodus, Leviticus, and Numbers—following the Hebrew headings: "Names" (Exod 1:1), "He-called" (Lev 1:1), and "In-the-wilderness" (Num 1:1). This is the great story of the exodus, in which the commandments are given. On the way, the reader is reminded of this over and over again. Three quotations: "At the third moon after the children of Israel had gone out of the land of Egypt" (Exod 19:1); "You shall not do as they do in the land of Egypt, where you lived" (Lev 18:3); and "After they had come out of the land of Egypt" (Num 1:1; 9:1; 33:38).

What do the surrounding books, Genesis and Deuteronomy, do to make up the five? From the creation of heaven and earth to the coffin of Joseph, waiting for the exodus in the last verse of the first book, Genesis tells us who that is, the main figure of the exodus: "Israel, my son, my firstborn" (Exod 4:22).

The first book of the Bible is about "Israel's firstbornship in the midst of the nations on earth." According to Breukelman this is "the theme of 'the book of the begettings of Adam, the human being'" (cf. Gen 5:1).

Two key moments stand out: Israel, representative of the whole of humankind, is the people that hands over *its* future to what *YHWH* sees (Gen 22:14), to what YHWH has in mind for his people's future (Abraham). And then, it is the people that receives its identity as "Israel" in the blessing of the unspoken Name (Jacob, Gen 32:22–32). Egypt, however, is already in view at key moments. In the promise of a son from his own body, for Abram, the people this "son" stands for is already characterized by the exodus: "Know this for certain, that your offspring shall be aliens in a land that is not theirs. They shall serve them [as slaves] there, and they shall be oppressed for four hundred years. . . . Afterwards they shall come out with great possessions" (Gen 15:13–14).

The exodus is prepared for in the story of Jacob. When he *goes down* to his son Joseph in Egypt, YHWH says to him: "I myself will *go down* with you to Egypt, and I will also *cause you to go up* again" (Gen 46:4). These words provide a background to what YHWH says to Moses at the time of his call: "I have *come down* . . . to *cause* my people *to go up* out of that land" (Exod 3:8). In the last chapter, when Joseph is comforting his brothers and speaking tenderly to them (cf. Isa 40:1), he adds this assurance: "God will surely come to you, he will cause you to go up out of this land." The reader is repeatedly reminded of this statement in Exodus (Exod 3:16; 4:31; 13:19).

The fifth book, Deuteronomy, consists of lengthy addresses by Moses. On the threshold of the Land (Deut 1:1; Num 36:13), just as the Israelites are about to cross the Jordan, he looks back on the exodus and forward to the future in the Land. He does this with what might be called an updating of the commandments that have been given—his last "words" (Devarim—the heading of the book in Hebrew), as he is speaking on the site where his grave is to be, in "the valley opposite Peor" (Deut 3:29; 34:6). There he will be buried by YHWH, so that there is no possibility of his grave being found and thus of him being venerated. One can only venerate Moses by obeying his "words." The last sight granted to Moses is a panorama view of the whole Land (Deut 34:1–4). Through Moses's eyes the reader sees the perspective of the exodus. His death brings the Torah to a close. After "Moses," the Prophets begin with Joshua.

3. Prophets: Exile

In the synagogue the Torah is read through in one year, Sabbath by Sabbath. Lections conclude in each case with passages from the Prophets. After Genesis 1:1–6:8, for instance, Isaiah 42:5–43:10 is read ("... I am YHWH, that is my name ... who created you, O Jacob, who formed you, O Israel," etc.) and after Genesis 23:1–25:19, the conclusion of the stories about Abraham, 1 Kings 1:1–31 (the last days of David and the selection of Solomon as his successor). The Torah stands in the center; the prophets form a ring around it. K. H. Miskotte attaches a canonical-hermeneutical value to the sequence of the three categories of the books in the TNK: the Torah is the central revelation of the Name. The Prophets contemporize the message of the Torah, impressing it upon the hearts of the listening community by narrating the history in the Land (Former Prophets) and preaching in religious, economic, and political situations (Latter Prophets). The Writings—the Psalms in particular—form the reaction of the listening community to the dual preaching. To some degree the sequence of the apostolic books, the New Testament, also corresponds to this: the Gospels to the Torah, Acts to the Former Prophets, and the Epistles to the Latter Prophets. A third category, the reaction of the community, is absent—although hymns are already beginning to appear in Revelation, for instance. One could also say, therefore, that the third category remains open for liturgical practice, first and foremost from the Psalms.

When speaking of the Prophets in this context we mean the Latter Prophets—as in common usage. In the meantime it is important to remember that the books from Joshua to Kings are also counted among the Prophets. But whenever the topic "Prophets: Exile" is addressed, the three major prophets and the twelve minor prophets are the ones concerned. Anyone surprised by this and moved to raise the objection, "But Isaiah lived around the year 700, a good century before Jerusalem was destroyed!" needs to bear in mind that we are not primarily talking about the "historical" person but about the book that bears his name. The book is usually divided into three: 1–39 First Isaiah, 40–55 Second Isaiah (Deutero-Isaiah) and 55–66 Third Isaiah (Trito-Isaiah). The first part repeatedly reflects historical situations from around the year 700; the second assumes the exile and the return; the third the history of the time after the return. It is now generally assumed that the book covers a period of a little over two centuries, with the time of the Babylonian captivity in the middle. In various details the opening chapter assumes the presence of Deutero- and Trito-Isaiah. One aspect of this is quite striking. We might imagine the book being read in a circle of pious people in the Second Temple period. There the words of "Isaiah" about the wayward people of the time *before* the exile resound (1:3–8): "An ox knows its owner, and the donkey its master's crib; but Israel does not know, my people do not understand. Ah, sinful nation. . . . Why do you seek further beatings? Why do you continue to rebel? The whole head is sick and the whole heart faint. . . . Your country lies desolate . . . turned upside-down [the word used specifically for Sodom and Gomorrah]. . . . Daughter Zion remained, like a booth in a vineyard, like a besieged city." Then the reader looks up and casts his eyes around the circle, as 1:9 is suddenly spoken in the "we"-form: "If YHWH of Hosts had not left *us* a few survivors, *we* would have been like Sodom, and become like Gomorrah." So they are now listening as a small group of survivors, following the account of Israel's "illness" in the prophecies. A terminal illness? Yes, but in the manner of Hezekiah, whose miraculous healing is related in a pivotal chapter (Isa 38) before the Book of Comfort that tells of Israel's restoration. However difficult circumstances may be for the returnees (cf. Isa 66:5), they can expect comfort, as from the book of comfort (Isa 40:1; 52:9). YHWH says: "As a mother comforts her child, so I will comfort you; you shall be comforted in Jerusalem" (Isa 66:13). The book of Isaiah is presented to us in the canon as *one* book. In all its diversity, it is based on the account of how people faced the exile but experienced the comfort of YHWH's mercy there, which made the return possible.

The book of Jeremiah is entirely concerned with the threat of exile and the provisional rescue of Jerusalem, at which point a first group of people were transported to Babylon with King Coniah/Jeconiah (e.g., Jer 22:24; cf. 28:1–4), and finally the definitive destruction of Jerusalem (Jer 39). The heart of this book too, however, is shaped by the promise of return (Jer 31).

In the book of Ezekiel the reader follows the events experienced by Jeremiah himself from a distance, as Ezekiel is among the first group of those taken to Babylon. As long as Jerusalem is not devastated, the hope of return is still alive for them. Ezekiel dashes this hope to the ground. This comes very graphically to expression in the piece of prophetic street theater that is described in Ezekiel 12:1–7. In the daytime Ezekiel prepares luggage for exile and places it outside. His audience is intrigued. What show is the prophet going to perform before them this time? They have to wait until dark. In the evening Ezekiel comes out, but in a rather odd way. He makes a hole in the mud wall of the house, climbs through it, loads the package on his shoulder and disappears into the dense darkness. "You shall cover your face, so that you may not see the 'Land,' for I have made you a 'sign' (symbol) for the house of Israel" (12:6). Thus reads God's commission. The pantomime is eloquent enough: through a breach cut in the wall of Jerusalem, the inhabitants will go into exile.

Nowhere in the Prophets is the return described more graphically than in the famous chapter of Ezekiel 37. "I shall open your graves, and bring you up from your graves, O my people. Then you shall *know that I am YHWH*" (Ezek 37:13). The last words form a refrain throughout the whole of the book. The whole event in this prophecy is a revelation of the Name.

The Twelve Prophets display great diversity. In this "book" we read, for example, the story of Jonah. Here too, however, the main concern is initially with the exile, in each case with the prospect of return (Hos 14:2–9; Amos 9:11–15; Obad 20; Mic 7:7–19, etc.). After the summary statement in Zephaniah 3:20, "At that time I will bring you home, at the time when I gather you; for I will make you renowned and praised among all the peoples of the earth, when I restore your fortunes before your eyes, says YHWH," in Haggai the reader is with the returnees. In Zechariah 10:6 YHWH can say retrospectively: "I will strengthen the house of Judah, and I will save the house of Joseph. I will bring them back because I have compassion on them, and they shall be as though I had not rejected them."

4. The Former Prophets

Buber calls the Former Prophets *Bücher der Geschichte* (books of history). After all, they recount Israel's history from the entry into the Land under Joshua up to the beginning of the exile. But it is not a kind of national history of Israel with a sad ending. The prophets speaking here have something to proclaim, and they do so using historical material, legends, fairy tale–like narratives (1 Sam 17), royal annals, and folkloristic prophet stories. Because in the canon they come before the three prophets and the twelve prophets, these books are called the "Former Prophets." They form the bridge between the Torah of Moses, the topic of the exodus from Egypt, and the "Latter" Prophets with the theme of the return from exile. They tell us next to nothing of the exile (see, however, Solomon's temple prayer in 1 Kgs 8:46–51). Nor, at the conclusion, is the return from Assyria or Babylon placed in prospect. This has been taken as evidence that the editing of these books must have taken place in Babylonian exile, otherwise the authors would surely have mentioned that great moment! Rather, what happens is that this topic is left to the Latter Prophets.

In a hidden way the return from exile is in fact sometimes assumed: for instance, in the motif of "the woman and her son." The *woman* points to Israel and the *son* to her future. It is not only in Ruth (in Writings, the third part of the TNK) that we come across this motif. There, Naomi is the childless widow (cf. Isa 54:1) who as "Israel" gains a son—that is, a future—through Ruth (Ruth 4:17). This motif also plays a part in the stories of Elijah and Elisha. In 2 Kings 8:1–6 the king is in conversation with Gehazi, the servant of Elisha, and asks him, "Tell me all the great things that Elisha has done." What story is Gehazi going to tell now? What is the great theme in prophecy? Prophetic words bring people to life. That is even the case with Elisha's bones. Gehazi cannot know this yet at this point, but the last thing that is related about the prophet is the incident in which people are startled by the approach of marauders during a funeral ceremony. The dead man is thrown unceremoniously into Elisha's grave and the people run away. "And as soon as the man touched the bones of Elisha, he came to life and stood on his feet" (2 Kgs 13:21). This is a splendid, typically biblical pronouncement in the form of an anecdote: prophecy brings life in the midst of death (cf. Ezek 37). Gehazi therefore summarizes *all* the great deeds for the king in the story of the raising to life of the deceased son of the Shunammite woman (2 Kgs 4:8–37). Now Elisha had said to this woman that she must leave the Land and go into exile, as a seven-year famine was on its way (cf. Ruth 1:1). At precisely the moment Gehazi is telling that story, she returns with her son (2 Kgs 8:5). She turns to the king, as the problem is now not with "the son" but with "the land": her house and her field. The king sees to it that she has it restored to her, because the material basis of the land is required for the future. To put it in the words of Ezekiel, YHWH "will place you on your own soil" (Ezek 37:14). The story thus gains the features of a parable about the proclamation of the Latter Prophets, the return from exile.

The Former Prophets, however, are not merely the historical bridge between exodus and exile, describing how the people abandoned YHWH and eventually threw away their freedom. Their own theme is the kingship in brotherhood, which finds form in David, and the building of the temple. After the giving of the Land under Joshua, the book of Judges works toward that messianic middle in the books of Samuel. The theme of kingship, identified with the name *David*, which also has an important place like this in the Psalms, is a factor that is given relatively marginal treatment in the Latter Prophets. We shall leave the prophetic proclamation about kingship and temple for a later volume (cf. my *Koning en Tempel*),[2] and concentrate here on exodus and exile. The Former Prophets end with the exile. The signal for a continuation of the history is confined to the

2 Editors' note: Karel Deurloo, Evert van den Berg, and Piet van Midden, *Koning en Tempel: Kleine Bijbelse Theologie deel II* (Kok: Kampen, 2004).

pardoning of Jehoiachin (Jeconiah), the king of Judah in Babylon (2 Kgs 25:27–30), but the event of the unexpected return is left until the second section of the Prophets.

In connection with the Former and Latter Prophets it is worth casting an eye over the genealogy in the first chapter of Matthew. The evangelist does not conduct "genealogical research" into the heritage of Jesus when he lists the forefathers—and the four special mothers. It is a good thing that we can compare it with Luke's list (3:23–38), which diverges from it considerably. Matthew *composes* his list with data from Scripture, taking some liberties. Thus he changes the name of King Asa (Matt 1:8; cf. 1 Kgs 15:9) to Asaph. Some translations "amend" this back to Asa (e.g., the Dutch NBG 1951), along with some manuscripts, thereby removing any link with the Psalms. The name of Amon (Matt 1:10; cf. 2 Kgs 21:19) also lends itself to a detailed sermon. Matthew drops one letter and makes this Amos, so that the prophets are also represented in the list. Fortunately, many modern translations keep Asaph and Amos, because this is a theological genealogy. The evangelist underlines this: "So all the generations from Abraham to *David* are fourteen generations [the numerical value of the name David in Hebrew is 4+6+4]; from David to the Babylonian deportation fourteen generations; and from the Babylonian deportation to the Messiah fourteen generations" (Matt 1:17). The fascinating thing is that Matthew is thus giving a view of the canon. Twice he points to a "middle": in relation to the Former Prophets, David; and in relation to the Latter Prophets, the Babylonian exile. But where is the Torah? It is as if the exodus has had to forfeit its place in the first 2×7. But doesn't everything begin with "who led you out of Egypt, out of the house of slavery"? As if the evangelist was expecting that question, he tells of the flight to Egypt. As a signal that his Gospel must be read from that perspective, at the beginning of the story about Jesus he places, as a fulfillment quotation, the word of YHWH: "Out of Egypt I called my son" (2:15). Matthew's Gospel amounts to a Passover/Easter story.

3
The Divine Name in the Exodus

Liberation theology finds its inspiration in the exodus. There are good reasons for this, but on the basis of the exodus it might perhaps be better to speak of emancipation theology. It is not without significance to note that the word *liberate* does not occur in the first thirteen chapters of the book of Exodus. In Exodus 6:6 we meet a whole series of verbs to describe YHWH's action with his people; in prime position "cause to move out" and then save, redeem, take as his people. The word *liberate* is absent. "YHWH your God" means, first and foremost, departure, heralded by the ten plagues, away from the Pharaonic system. The people are mobilized by the Pesach "service," the night of watching, which leads into the departure. The Passover meal is eaten hastily, one's loins girded, shoes on one's feet, staff in one's hand (Exod 12:11). Meanwhile Egypt takes a hit to its firstborn, the strength of its future, so that Pharaoh now says: "Rise up, go away from my people!" (Exod 12:31). Celebrating the feast of mazzot, unleavened bread, Israel sets out. "The people took their dough before it was leavened, with their kneading-bowls wrapped up in their cloaks on their shoulders" (Exod 12:34). It is a liturgical story and a story for the worship service, the liturgy of Pesach. The reader has to wait for the word *liberate* until the end of the first part that deals with Egypt: the story of the Reed Sea.

Although it is repeatedly said that YHWH causes his people *to go* up from Egypt (Deut 20:1; 1 Sam 10:18; Jer 2:6; Amos 2:10; Ps 81:10), the primary and most common word is "move out." This word constantly reminds Israel of its departure point. When Moses describes the whole exodus from Egypt up to the Land, the words used are "These are the stages by which the Israelites *went out* of the land of Egypt. . . . Moses wrote down their *starting points*, stage by stage, by command of the Lord, and these are the stages according to their *starting places*: They set out from Rameses in the first month, on the day after the Passover the Israelites moved out boldly in the sight of all the Egyptians." Then follows the summary: "They set out. . . . they set out. . . . until they camped in the plains of Moab by the Jordan at Jericho" (Num 33:1–48). The departure point is the Pesach festival in Egypt at Rameses. This geographical place name occurs only in four passages. As father Israel and his sons come to Egypt, the land of Goshen is allocated to them. That is where they settle; it is there that Joseph meets his father (Gen 46:28). In Genesis 47:11 it is already called Rameses (anachronistically, for literary purposes). It is the borderland from where it is easy to set out for Canaan. Here the people build the supply cities, Pithom and "Rameses" for Pharaoh—one might think of outpost bases for military operations (cf. Exod 14:6–7)—under conditions of forced labor (Exod 1:11). Rameses means "forced labor." But also Pesach: this is where the exodus from Egypt begins: "I am YHWH, and I will cause you to move out from the forced labor [NRSV: burdens] of the Egyptians" (Exod 6:6). With their unleavened bread and their bakers' troughs on their shoulders, "the Israelites journeyed from Rameses to Succoth, about six hundred thousand men on foot, besides children" (Exod 12:37).

1. Moving Out and Going Up

It was YHWH who, through Moses, caused Israel to move out. In these two names the exodus has a vertical aspect and a horizontal aspect. In the call of Moses this is given contour in a special way. When YHWH addresses Moses, he doesn't say "I am YHWH" but "I am the God of your father," which is subsequently complemented with "the God of Abraham, the God of Isaac, and the God of Jacob" (Exod 3:6). The divine Name has already occurred in this story, but only on the level of the reader. Moses hears only the word *God* until the name is revealed to him in a special way. The Name YHWH is therefore absent in the first two chapters of the book as well. That Name is hinted at from as far back as Genesis 39 (except for Gen 49:18). To Joseph the brothers call themselves "servants of *the God of your father*." That is also what Israel's God calls himself in his last revelation in night visions: "Jacob, Jacob . . . I am God, the God of your father . . ." (Gen 46:2; cf. 49:25). The same phrasing occurs here too: "Moses, Moses . . . I am the God of your father" (Exod 3:4, 6). That this is a reminder of the revelation to father Israel is confirmed by these words: "Do not be afraid to go down to Egypt, for I will go down with you to Egypt, and I will also bring you up [cause you to go up] again" (Gen 46:3, 4). The "going down" in particular needs to be heard not only in connection with Abram (Gen 12:10) and Isaac (Gen 26:2) but also against the background of Jacob's lament over Joseph's supposed death: "I will go down to the realm of the dead to my son, mourning" (Gen 37:35). This realm of the dead, and the house of slavery, turns out to be Egypt. Just before going down, Jacob says: "Enough! My son is still alive. I must go and see him before I die" (Gen 45:28). In Egypt, Jacob's descendants will, it should be noted, "live and not die" (Gen 42:2; 43:8; cf. 47:19; 50:20) on account of the divine promise to Jacob. At his call, Moses hears the words spoken to Jacob: "I have *come down* to deliver them [my people] from the Egyptians and to make them *go up* to a land flowing with milk and honey" (Exod 3:8). In this context one might quote, "YHWH causes to go down to the realm of the dead and to go up out of it" (1 Sam 2:6). How does he do this in Egypt? The motivation is splendidly prepared in the introduction. When Israel sighs and cries out from its slavery, its cry for help just rises *up*, to "God." "God heard their groaning, and God remembered his covenant with Abraham, Isaac, and Jacob. God looked upon the Israelites, and God took notice of them" (Exod 2:24). YHWH now speaks to Moses: "I have *observed* the misery of *my* people [this is the first time this occurs!] who are in Egypt; I have *heard* their cry on account of their taskmasters. Indeed I *know* their sufferings, and I have come down" (Exod 3:7–8). YHWH knew their suffering and made it his own business. But how will he cause them to go up out of the Land? How will the vertical movement be changed into a horizontal one? The point of YHWH's speech to Moses is given with a double "and now . . ." In the first, words are again cited from the introduction: "And now, behold, the cry of the Israelites has come to me and I have also seen how the Egyptians oppress them." What does YHWH do? "And now, I will send you to Pharaoh. Cause my people, the Israelites, to *move out*" (Exod 3:10). That is how it will be in the rest of the story, too. Moses causes them to move out (Exod 3:12) while YHWH causes them to go up out of the misery of Egypt (Exod 3:17). This emphasizes the seriousness of Moses's answer: "Who am I that I should go to Pharaoh, and cause the Israelites to move out of Egypt?" (Exod 3:11).

2. The Name Occurs in "God"

The four letters YHWH are not holy in themselves. In ancient extrabiblical texts this name occurs mainly in blessing and curse texts, although it is not always certain whether these are Israelite or not. YHWH is sometimes listed among other gods and goddesses. Sometimes as a male (!) divinity he also has a female consort, not only in the eighth century but also as late as the fifth. The prayer "hallowed be your Name" cannot thus relate to the occurrence—wherever that might be—of the four letters, but to the telling and proclaiming of the Name in the Scriptures. The last sentence of Genesis 4, before the book proper begins in 5:1, reads programmatically: "At that time people began to invoke the name of YHWH" (Gen 4:26). That happens in Israel. As an example, Abram proclaims the Name when he arrives at the exact center of the Land of Canaan (Gen 12:8). The modern reader is therefore amazed that YHWH says to Moses, "I am YHWH. I appeared to Abraham, Isaac, and Jacob as 'God-Shaddai' [cf. Gen

19:1; 28:3; 35:11], but by my name YHWH I did not make myself known to them" (Exod 6:2). This sentence was an argument for the "documentary hypothesis" in Genesis, because its author was said to have had a form of the book in front of him in which YHWH did not appear by name, but Shaddai did instead. We are in the dark about the meaning of this name, although it is commonly translated as "Almighty." But how should this sentence be understood in the context of Exodus 6? This has to be a backward glance to the story of Moses's call, which gives an account of the crucial revelation of the meaning of the Name. That's not how YHWH was known to the patriarchs, even if the reader of the stories will immediately associate that Name in Genesis with Exodus 3 and 4. The impact of the latter (Exod 6:2) is subsequently all the greater in view of what is revealed there.

The Name is imprinted upon Moses from the start, when he has to answer the question of who has sent him with the words: "*I Am* has sent me to you" (Exod 3:14). "I am" is something that really only YHWH himself can say: "I am who I am." Is the first or the second "I am" meant in Moses's answer? Either way, it is spoken in the godforsaken environment of the enslaved people. Just look again at Exodus 1 and 2. The little word *God* occurs only indirectly in Exodus 1:17 and following. The undirected cries from the depths of servitude rise and thus still reach "God" (Exod 2:23). Who is "I am"? Anyone translating the Hebrew will know the word does not mean "the one who is." He or she can also render "I am who I am" with "I am as I will be there." Isn't that how the second "I am" in Moses's answer should be taken? "I-shall-be-there has sent me to you"? Isn't this the unveiling of "the peculiar character of the divine Name" (Cok den Hertog)?[1] In Moses's mission, YHWH will be there for his people, he will be at their side. In introducing the revelation of the Name, YHWH said to Moses: "*I am with* you; and this shall be the sign for you that it is

1 Editors' note: Cok den Hertog, "Het zonderlinge karakter van de godsnaam: literaire, psychoanalytische en theologische aspecten van het roepingsverhaal van Mozes (Exodus 2.23–4.17)" (PhD thesis, University of Amsterdam, 1996).

I who sent you: when you have caused the people to move out of Egypt, you shall worship God on this mountain" (Exod 3:12; the mountain was the site of Moses's call and the giving of the Ten Commandments). From the outset YHWH's being-there is colored by the exodus and the covenant on Sinai. Through Moses the people—and thus the hearers of the text—are already addressed: You! That is how YHWH will be there, *with* Moses. That is how Moses is sent to bring about YHWH's promise that he will cause his people to go up in the move out of Egypt. So this mission is essential. When Moses says he is not a man of words (Exod 4:10)—just like Jeremiah when he is commissioned (Jer 1:6)—he is told how the Name "I will be there" will be manifested: "And now *go*, and *I* will *be there* with your mouth and *teach* you what you are to speak." Then comes the word with which he refuses his commissioning in the customary eastern manner: "O my Lord, please send by the hand of him you will send" (NRSV: "please send someone else," Exod 4:13). The anger of YHWH is kindled against Moses, and he confronts him with the fait accompli that his brother Aaron, who has speaking ability, has already "moved out" to meet him: "You shall speak to him and put the words in his mouth." Isn't this what YHWH does with his prophets (e.g., Jer 1:9)? What role is being assigned to Moses here? How will YHWH's "being-there" play out? "I myself *will be there* with your mouth and with his mouth, and will *teach* you (cf. Torah) what you shall do." Aaron will speak to the people on Moses's behalf; and then comes the amazing sentence: "He shall serve as a mouth for you, and you shall serve as God for him" (Exod 4:16).

Does "God" exist? He is there with his Name, he occurs as YHWH in Moses who must play the part of God. YHWH will thus cause his people to go up out of Egypt through the mission that Moses must carry out: I am with you, and you will cause my people to move out. The voice will therefore speak on Sinai: "I am YHWH your God, who caused you to move out from the land of Egypt, from the house of servitude." From the perspective of biblical theology this is where it all begins. To say "Israel" is from the outset to say "exodus." It begins in Rameses, after the Passover meal, but that beginning is grounded in the divine Name, which is accomplished in the mission of Moses, as "God" on earth, on the mountain of God (Exod 3:1). How could it be any clearer that YHWH fully and completely defines the word "God"?

3. Service of God and Servitude in Slavery

How did Egypt become the "house of servitude," the "house of slavery"? Through Joseph. Just like the patriarchs, he too has his dark side. He suffers from Egyptian assimilation. That was already apparent at an earlier point, when Pharaoh appointed him as the highest Egyptian official (Gen 41:46–57), but it becomes acute in Genesis 47:13–26 when he brings the whole Egyptian population into slavery during the famine. First he manages to separate the Egyptians from their money and then from their possessions. When they shout to him roughly in a popular uprising "Give us bread!" he responds tit for tat: "Give me your livestock." And they come with all their horses—we are in Egypt!—their sheep and cattle and all their donkeys. And so Joseph steers them through that year of famine. In the second year they take a different tone: "We cannot hide from my lord that our money is all spent. . . . There is nothing left in the sight of my lord but our bodies and our lands. Shall we die before your eyes, both we and our land? Buy us and our land in exchange for bread. We with our land will become slaves for Pharaoh" (Gen 47:18–19). Joseph takes harsh measures. He removes the people from the fields and brings them across to the cities "from one end of Egypt to the other" (47:21). So from now on the Egyptians will have to toil away as serfs on Pharaoh's fields. They even express their gratitude for this: "You have saved our lives; may it please my lord, we will be slaves to Pharaoh!" (47:25).

Egypt, to where Joseph himself had been sold as a slave, has definitely become a "house of slavery" through Pharaoh's official. But around this story something else is related: Joseph gave land to his father's house and provided it with bread (Gen 47:11; 47:27). Israel is free in the land of slavery. Why does this story of the "house of servitude" have to be told? To provide a background for the conclusion of Genesis. Jacob dies and is buried by his sons in Machpelah (Gen 49:29–50:14). It now occurs to Joseph's brothers that the special position they enjoy as a result of Joseph's provision is exclusively due to Joseph's special link with his father and that out of revenge for what they did to him earlier he could easily take that privileged position away from them at any point. Then they would become slaves of Pharaoh just like the Egyptians. With an appeal to a "last will" of their father, Jacob, known only to them, they turn to Joseph through a messenger. They choose their words carefully and opt for a liturgical style as if it were a prayer. In addition they try to touch the most sensitive part of Joseph's heart with their first and last words:

> *Your father* gave us this instruction before he died:
> "You must say to Joseph:
> I beg you, forgive the crime of your brothers
> and the wrong they did in harming you."
> And now:
> therefore please forgive the crime
> of the servants of the God of *your father*! (Gen 50:16–17)

After this message the brothers come in person and fall before Joseph with the words: "We are here as your slaves/servants." They had previously used the well-considered wording we, "the servants/slaves of the God of your father." Joseph had to hear this loud and clear! They are not Egyptians. They serve YHWH. The Name itself remains unmentioned but is referred to as "the God of your father." The narrator is referring to two important texts that were also noted above under section 1 ("Moving Out and Going Up"). This is the God who goes down with them to Egypt and causes them to go up from there (Gen 46:2–4; Exod 3:8). Surely Joseph can't treat his brothers, who serve this God, as servants/slaves of Pharaoh (Gen 47:25)? But if so, it would be better to be slaves of Joseph!

Joseph answers that he is not standing in God's place and that God has clearly already forgiven them by "preserving a numerous people" in the land of death and slavery. All Joseph wants to do is to follow God's example and implicitly grant them forgiveness by continuing to provide for them. "In this way he reassured them, speaking kindly to them" (Gen 50:21). It is no coincidence that this is a combination of words that is used in the prophets for the start of the return from exile (Isa 40:1; Hos 2:14). Joseph's last words offer a prospect of exodus from Egypt: "I am about to die; but God will surely come to you, and cause you to go up out of this land to the land that he swore to Abraham, to Isaac and to Jacob" (Gen 50:24; cf. 3:16). The whole of Genesis is thus presented in the light of the exodus. The coffin in which Joseph's embalmed body is laid is, in the last sentence of Genesis, the last visible sign of this, as Joseph, in the very land of graves (cf. Exod 14:11), is not buried in a grave but remains to await the exodus (Exod 13:19).

But a new king arises over Egypt, who has not known Joseph (Exod 1:8). The Egyptians then make the children of Israel slaves, making their lives bitter "with hard service in mortar and brick and in every kind of field labor. All the slave labor imposed on them was accompanied by mistreatment" (Exod 1:14). Five times we hear the root *abad* (be a slave/serve) in a single sentence. Things go on as before. Could a new period break in with a new Pharaoh coming to the throne? In the time of Moses? "In those many days the king of Egypt died, but the Israelites continued to sigh from their servitude and they cried out"—until God hears, sees, and knows them (Exod 2:23–25), until he goes down to cause them to go up (Exod 3:8). At his call on Horeb, Moses is given a sign: the people will *serve* God on this mountain. A new religion? No, a new service of God, in which the people of YHWH are free, having moved out from the house of servitude where Pharaoh, the representative of the super state power, disposing over life and death like a god (Exod 1:15–22), is in charge. YHWH's order that Moses must speak to Pharaoh in Exodus 7:16 echoes almost as a refrain in the following chapters: "Let my people go to *serve* me in the wilderness!" However, that service begins already as liturgy in Egypt with the institution of the Passover meal (Exod 12). "Moses said to the people, 'Remember this day on which you moved out of Egypt, out of the house of slavery. . . . Today, in the month of Abib, you are moving out. It must be as when YHWH let you arrive in the Land . . . then you shall keep this service in this month'" (Exod 13:3–5). This is a "catechetical" feast, because when the children ask, "What do you mean by this service?" (Exod 12:26), the story of the exodus must be told.

And the sign to Moses, this "serving God on this mountain"? This reaches its climax in the giving of the Torah, of the Ten Commandments and the building of the tabernacle. YHWH, Israel's God, who caused his people to move out from the house of servitude, speaks: "You shall have no other divinity before my face [contrary to my attentive and familiar presence]. . . . You shall not bow down to them nor *serve* them" (Exod 20:3, 5), nor, more precisely translated, "be made serviceable to them," let yourselves be brought into their coercive and belittling cult. Instead of freedom it would be once again a "house of servitude"; and that surely is the incomparable thing about Israel, that it has been redeemed from this. David expresses it in his prayer like this:

> Great are you, my lord YHWH
> indeed, no one is like you,
> no God besides you,
> according to all that we have heard with our ears.
> And who is like your people, like Israel,
> the only nation on earth
> for which a deity went
> to redeem it as a people,
> to make a Name for himself,
> by performing this great deed for them,
> awesome deeds for your land,
> with an eye on your people
> that you redeemed for yourself out of Egypt:
> nations and its gods. (2 Sam 7:22–23)

With the exodus YHWH made a Name for himself in Israel: "I am your-God-alone, who caused you to move out from the land of Egypt, out from the house of servitude."

4. Exodus and Liberation

"Who caused you to move out." In the translations (e.g., at Exod 13:9) we read "who brought you out" (NRSV, NIV, GNT, cf. AV). There is nothing wrong with this of course. There are worse translations. In French it is perhaps easier: "qui t'ai fait sortir" (TOB). This preserves an aspect that is of some significance in the translation. In relation to the move, it holds together the departure of the people and YHWH's causing the departure. For to say that YHWH caused his people to move out from the house of servitude implies that "you moved out of the house of servitude" (Exod 13:3). You were actively involved in this yourselves.

On the basis of the sentence introducing the Ten Commandments, Kroon and Miskotte are right to summarize the commandments themselves in the single sentence: Stay with your deliverer! In the repeated "You shall not" the great positive is the heart of the matter: the freedom you have been delivered into. Each "You shall not" aims to protect this freedom against the threat that people will start serving idols once again. Murder, theft, and so on are infringements of this freedom. The "No" is spoken for the sake of the resounding "Yes!"—the freedom YHWH has placed you in. Stay with your deliverer! True as this is, in TNK the exodus is never described as liberation but as moving out, causing to move out. It begins with the celebration of Passover. The people themselves have to do this (Exod 12) and thus make a start with moving out. As they celebrate the feast, people find they belong. All the children of Israel did as YHWH had commanded Moses and Aaron; that's what they did. And it happened that very day: "YHWH caused the Israelites to move out from the land of Egypt, company by company" (Exod 12:50–51). The last word suggests that there would subsequently be fighting, but for the time being that is not the case. On the contrary, when "Pharaoh let the people go, God did not lead them by way of the land of the Philistines, although that was nearer." The reference is to the route along the Mediterranean Sea, which forms the normal connection between Egypt and Canaan. But that's precisely where you would come up against the Philistines living in the southwest of that land. "God did not lead them by way of the land of the Philistines . . . for God said: 'If the people have to face war (with the Philistines), they may change their minds and return to Egypt.' For that reason God led the people by the roundabout way of the wilderness toward the Reed Sea. The children of Israel went up out of the land of Egypt prepared for battle" (Exod 13:17–18). But it is precisely at the Reed Sea that the great holy war will be fought. Up against the Reed Sea, the people are hemmed in by Pharaoh's pursuing army. War? Well yes, but it will be the holy war par excellence, the "war to end all wars." On this site YHWH will show his glory to Pharaoh and all his military might, so that they "shall know that I am YHWH" (Exod 14:4). Moses allays the panic of the people with the words "Do not be afraid, stand firm, and see the deliverance that YHWH will accomplish for you today; for the Egyptians whom you see today you shall never see again. YHWH will fight for you, and you have only to keep still" (Exod 14:13–14). The only thing the people have to do—though armed for a fight!—is to walk across the sea on the dry part in the middle. "Thus YHWH saved Israel that day from the Egyptians" (Exod 14:30). And Moses sang: "YHWH is a warrior; YHWH is his name!" (Exod 15:3). As YHWH says: Vengeance is mine . . . and not yours, so you in relation to this story could adapt this to, War is mine. It is YHWH who "makes wars cease to the end of the earth" (Ps 46:9).

Immediately following the exodus, the first exemplary liberation occurs. After the exodus the Name of YHWH is proclaimed as the liberator. Hosea puts it appropriately: YHWH says, "I have been YHWH your God from the land of Egypt; you know no God but me, and besides me there is no savior" (Hos 13:4). From the land of Egypt onward, a history of liberations develops—liberations that occur for Israel, beginning with the liberation at the Reed Sea. This is an act of sheer benevolence on God's part, in which Israel is only present as the one for whom the act is performed: "You, keep still!" It's different at the initial departure. Then the people are present, "there," just as Moses is "there" at his call. He is also "there" in the sense that he is, as it were, arrested by

YHWH, but he is arrested in order to do something himself too. YHWH causes his people to "go up" out of Egypt as Moses causes them to "move out." Thus YHWH causes his people to move out in the event in which they themselves move out as well. "Remember this day on which you move out of Egypt, out of the house of servitude, because YHWH causes you to move out of there by strength of hand" (Exod 13:3). Only by doing that did the people get to know YHWH. "I will be there, *just as I will be there*." The latter has to be experienced. Anyone who does not go the way of the exodus, who does not live through or experience the story of the exodus, does not know who YHWH is. Anyone who does not practice the Ten Commandments will not know what the divine Name means. Granted, the covenant the people enter into is not the same as the one that was agreed by Israel, but the people still must answer, "We will do it, we will hear it" (Exod 24:7).

Who is YHWH? Who can say what is inherent in the divine Name? Only the people that submit themselves to the exodus and indeed participate in it. In this context one might do well to recall one of Calvin's statements: "All right knowledge of God is born of obedience."[2] Hence the remarkable sequence: we will do it, we will hear it. Only one who does it has truly heard it. The mystery of the coming into being of the divine Name can therefore be expressed with the call "Hear O Israel, YHWH is our God." And the hearer can add "YHWH is one," he alone is our God and no other (Deut 6:4). Moving out is commitment, it is keeping the commandments: setting up no other god before his face. Not making any image of divine power, with the aim of entering into its service, not using the Name YHWH for things and authorities that have nothing to do with that Name as the event of the exodus does. That means not exploiting your time as if there were no end to your work and your achievements. YHWH will also be present in the limitation of your impassioned working week. And those who were there before you and who point to the exodus, you shall

2 Editors' note: John Calvin, *Institutes of the Christian Religion*, ed. J. T. McNeill, trans. F. L. Battles, 2 vols. (Philadelphia: Westminster, 1960), 1.6.2.

honor. And then the person you come into contact with or have to deal with: you shall not take his life, you shall not take away his partner, you shall not take away his material basis of life, you shall not take away his good name. You yourself shall not desire to be your "neighbor," to be in his position. You are the one who moved out of Egypt and thereby came to know YHWH, whose first move is to say, "I am YHWH your God, who caused you to move out of Egypt."

This incomplete and rather breathless paraphrase of the Ten Commandments is given here simply in order to emphasize the extent to which knowing the Name is predicated upon involvement in the exodus: "I am YHWH your God, sanctify yourself and be holy, for I am holy. . . . I am YHWH, who caused you to go up out of the land of Egypt, to be God for you. Be holy for I am holy" (Lev 11:44–45). When Hosea, alluding to the Ten Commandments, writes "Swearing, lying, and murder; and stealing and adultery break out; bloodshed follows bloodshed!" he introduces this sentence with "There is no faithfulness or loyalty, and no *knowledge of God* in the Land" (Hos 4:1–2).

YHWH is God, and you can only get to know the "happening" divine Name by hearing and participating in the history of the exodus. *Moving out* is the primordial word for Israel.

The theme of the Exodus is the central datum of the Torah that is to be proclaimed. All are called to this:

> O give thanks to YHWH,
> *call on his Name,*
> make known his deeds among the peoples!
> (Ps 105:1)

How do you do that? In this psalm it happens by recounting a song about the exodus. When Daniel prays in the distress of the exile, he says as he gets to the heart of the matter in his petition, "And now, O Lord our God, who caused your people to move out of the land of Egypt with a mighty hand and made your Name renowned even to this day. . . . O Lord, hear. O Lord, forgive. O Lord, listen!" (Dan 9:15, 19). It is on the basis of his Name in the exodus that his Name is called upon in the exile.

4
The Giving of the Torah and the Land

YHWH came down in order to cause his people to go up to the Land overflowing with milk and honey, and he achieves this by sending Moses to Pharaoh to cause his people to move out. The latter phrase is used dozens of times to confront hearers with YHWH. However frequently the phrase "cause to go up out of Egypt" occurs in the Former and Latter Prophets, particularly in the book of Jeremiah, in the book of Exodus it is found only in the story of the golden calf, and even there, only in special connection with Moses (see chapter 6, section 3).

YHWH will cause the people to go up *to the Land*. The commission to Moses does not speak of any "bringing to the Land." YHWH answers Moses's objection, "Who am I?" with the divine Name: I will be with you; and with the sign that will only be accomplished in the future: "You shall serve God on this mountain" (Exod 3:12). This sign, as we shall see, will typify Moses. "Causing to come into/bringing to the Land" is not granted to Moses. It is, however, said more than twenty times of YHWH in the Torah (cf. Exod 6:7). It is the completion of the narrative explanation of the Name; but this too is achieved in the ministry of a human being: YHWH "commissioned Joshua son of Nun and said, 'Be strong and bold, for you shall cause the children of Israel to come into the Land that I promised them by oath.'" And then YHWH speaks as he spoke to Moses: "And I will be with you" (Deut 31:23).

1. The Jordan Flows Between the Torah and the Prophets

Mount Horeb, the place where Moses's call takes place, will turn out to be Sinai, the mountain of the Torah. In reference to this the narrator drops the word *senê*, "thorn bush," five times (Exod 3:2–4). The great middle section of the books of Moses plays out at Mount Sinai (Exodus 19–Numbers 10). Moses is the prime speaking and acting figure there. However much he dominates the entire story, in Egypt, in the wilderness, on Sinai and—especially in Deuteronomy—"in the plains of Moab by the Jordan at Jericho" (Num 36:13), he will not cross the Jordan to let the people inherit the Land.

In the book of Numbers "the other side of the Jordan at Jericho" is the last stopping place on the journey from Egypt to the Land (Num 22:1; 26:3, 63, etc.). It is made clear to Reuben, Gad, and the half tribe of Manasseh, the Transjordanian tribes, that they too must have a share in the gift of the Land by *crossing over the Jordan* with their brothers, because this will introduce the new period in the Land that YHWH is giving them for their possession (Num 33:50–56). This theme is especially emphasized in the book of Deuteronomy. At this last stopping place "on the other side of the Jordan, in the wilderness," Moses began to expound this Torah (the book of Deuteronomy) (Deut 1:1–5) with a view to life in the Land after the crossing of the Jordan (9:1). That life will only be possible with this Torah (11:31–32). After the crossing of the Jordan the Torah will be visibly present in writing (27:2, 4). In the rest that will be given after the crossing, the people will act in accordance with what Moses has commanded, and they will rejoice before God's face (12:10–12). If Israel does not do this after crossing, it will not live in the Land for long (30:18). In short, "through this [word] you may live long in the Land that you are crossing over the Jordan to possess" (32:47). The book of Deuteronomy, however, concludes with the fact that Moses does not cross the Jordan. His death is the completion of the Torah. Moses holds his speech on the site of his tomb, in "the valley opposite Beth-Peor" (3:29; 34:6). What is the reason for this? Moses himself, it should be noted, had prayed: "O Lord, YHWH, you have only begun to let your servant *see* your greatness and your might; what god in heaven or on earth can perform deeds and mighty acts like yours?" (i.e., the exodus). Moses continues: "Let me cross over to *see* the good Land beyond the Jordan . . . but YHWH was angry with me [in Hebrew a word-play on 'cross over'] on your account and would not heed me. YHWH said to me, 'Enough from you! Never speak to me of this matter again!'" He was not permitted to cross over, but he was granted the opportunity to *see* the Land from the top of Pisgah (Deut 3:23–27; cf. 1:37; 4:21–24). The text presupposes the one moment of Moses's transgression but does not make that explicit here: he struck the rock for water instead of speaking to the rock as he was instructed to do (Num 20:2–13; 27:12–14). It is all the more striking that the anger is spelled out with the words "on your account." How does the people benefit from Moses's death? What else could it be than that Moses now needs to write down the spoken words of the Torah (Deut 31:9) so as to be able to give the book to the people when they cross the Jordan, for their new time in the Land?

There is in fact an explicit reminder of Moses's own disobedience in the last commandment to him (Deut 32:48–52), to highlight the obedience of his last deed. "Ascend this mountain . . . view the Land of Canaan . . . and die there on the mountain that you ascend." Moses does as he is told: "Then Moses went up from the plains of Moab to Mount Nebo, to the top of Pisgah, which is opposite Jericho, and YHWH showed him the whole Land. . . . YHWH said to him, 'This is the land of which I swore to Abraham, to Isaac, and to Jacob, saying, "I will give it to your descendants"; I have let you see it with your eyes, but you shall not cross over there'" (Deut 34:1–4). Then Moses's death will be his act of obedience. "Then Moses, the servant of YHWH, died there in the land of Moab, at YHWH's command. He buried him in the valley in the land of Moab, opposite Beth-peor [cf. 3:29]. No one knows his burial place to this day" (34:5–6). Not only should Moses's grave not become a bone of contention between Judah and the Northern Kingdom of Israel, but it must—lying in Moab—remain undiscoverable, because veneration of Moses should not be directed to his grave but only to the words spoken by him. A similar thing will happen with the *prophet* Elijah (2 Kgs 2). These words will function in the first book of the Former Prophets: "After the death of Moses the servant of YHWH, YHWH spoke to Joshua son of Nun, Moses's assistant, saying, 'My servant Moses is dead. Now proceed to cross the Jordan . . . . This book of the Torah [written by Moses—Deut 17:18; 31:24] shall not depart out of your mouth'" (Josh 1:1–8). The written words live as they are spoken. Only thus will the paths into the land be prosperous.

The Name of YHWH is told in the exodus out of Egypt and the entry into the Land. "I am YHWH your God, who causes you to move out" (cf. Exod 6:7–8). The one Name is borne out in two names, in the person and work of Moses but also of Joshua. Moses is not permitted to complete the great work. He functions in the crucial beginning of it; Joshua will stand at the head of the crossing (Deut 3:24–28), but once again the word is "YHWH your God himself will cross over before you" (Deut 31:3). This occurs as Joshua "causes the people to come into the Land" (31:23). Then, after the crossing of the Jordan, the Torah will function "prophetically."

2. Moses and Joshua

By the bush in the wilderness, the *senê* that burns but is not consumed, which calls to mind Mount Sinai, Moses hears:

> Come no closer!
> Remove the sandals from your feet
> for the place on which you are standing is holy ground.
> (Exod 3:5)

and then:

> This shall be the sign for you that it is I who sent you:
> when you have caused the people to move out,
> you shall serve God on this mountain. (Exod 3:12)

The exodus began at Passover. When do they arrive at the mountain? In the third month, *on that very day* (Exod 19:1). This is the expression for a feast day, but we are not told which one. The most likely candidate would be Shavuoth, Pentecost, the feast at which the synagogue celebrates the giving of the Torah. The people must not climb this sacred site, the mountain, nor even touch it with a foot. An enigmatic sentence then follows: "When the *yobêl* [horn] sounds a long blast, they may go up on the mountain" (Exod 19:13). We know this *yobêl* from the so-called Jubilee year. In the same way as the days are counted from Passover to "Pentecost," the fiftieth day of the Feast of Weeks, so too are the years counted from the giving of the Land under Joshua. Whatever has been done with the property, in the fiftieth year the *yobêl* sounds; then everyone is allowed to return to the field as distributed under Joshua (Lev 25). But what is the *yobêl* doing here, on Sinai? Nothing. There is no talk yet of a "long blast sounding." No one climbs the mountain, except for Moses, for the giving of the Torah. Sinai thus remains the holy mountain of YHWH, but the *yobêl* that is not heard here points to the future.

In the book that bears his name, Joshua is described in various ways that make him similar to Moses. The most striking parallel is the crossing of the Jordan on dry land, just like the crossing of the Reed Sea. "On that day YHWH exalted Joshua in the sight of all Israel; and they stood in awe of him, as they had stood in awe of Moses, all the days of his life" (Josh 4:14). Equally appropriate, however, is the following:

> It happened, when Joshua was in Jericho,
> he looked up and saw
> a man standing before him,
> with a drawn sword in his hand.
> Joshua went to him and said to him,
> "Are you one of us, or one of our adversaries?"
> He replied,
> "Neither;
> but as commander of the army of YHWH
> I have now come."

> Joshua fell on his face to the earth
> and worshipped, and he said to him,
> "What do you command your servant, my lord?"
> The commander of the army of YHWH said to Joshua,
> "Remove the sandals from your feet,
> for the place where you stand is holy."
> And Joshua did so. (Josh 5:13–15)

Was Joshua standing *in* Jericho? Many translators have found that so strange that they have made it "by/near Jericho," forgetting that biblical authors deal with what we call history or geography in their own special way. At the beginning of the second chapter Joshua gave the spies the assignment: "Go, view the Land, [namely] Jericho." They make their observations only in Jericho, but in their report they say, "YHWH has given *all the Land* into our hands" (Josh 2:24). So the reader may conclude that Jericho stands for the Land, *pars pro toto*. Just as Moses stood previously by the burning bush on the holy mountain to which he would bring the people to worship God, so too Joshua stood here already in the holy Land where he will bring the people to possess it. Here too the account begins with Passover (Josh 5:10–12), and the story of the giving of Jericho reminds the reader of Shavuoth/Pentecost by virtue of the use of the number seven—for instance, seven priests with seven horns; on the seventh day the people walk around Jericho seven times. No one may set foot on the holy mountain, which is the mountain of YHWH. That is the site of the *giving of the Torah*. It is permitted to set foot on the "holy Land"—"the place where you are standing is holy"—the Land of YHWH (cf. Lev 25:23), because this is now about the *giving of the Land*. "When they make a long blast with the *yobêl*-horn . . . the wall of the city falls down flat, and all the people go up, straight ahead" (Josh 6:5) into "Jericho." As the heart and soul of the exodus these two things belong inseparably together, Torah and Land. The Torah is given to point the "way" to be followed into the Land. The Torah tells us that the Land is given. "See, I have set the Land before you" (Deut 1:8), we hear constantly. Each step along the way as they enter the Land, they mutter, mindful of the Torah, "given!" "Every place that the sole of your foot will tread upon I have given to you, as I promised to Moses" (Josh 1:3). And so we move from the hearing of the Torah to prophetic practice in the first book of the Former Prophets. The exodus that YHWH began with Moses he completes with Joshua, whose name means "YHWH delivers."

3. From Generation to Generation

The story of the exodus is full of critical moments. Even before the crossing of the Reed Sea, as Pharaoh's army is approaching, the exodus people cry out to Moses, "Was it because there were no graves in Egypt [Egypt of course being famous for its tombs and pyramids] that you have taken us away to die in the wilderness? What have you done to us, causing us to move out of Egypt?" (Exod 14:11). And so it continues as far as the plains of Moab by the Jordan. They would rather run after the supreme deity Baal-Peor than stay with YHWH (Deut 14:1–4; cf. Num 25). The two great critical moments, however, are the story of the golden calf (see chapter 6, section 3) and the story of the spies. The latter divides the people into two age generations: the older generation, which left Egypt and dies in the wilderness, and the new one, which was born in the wilderness and is entering the Land (Josh 5:2–9). The twelve spies, one to represent each tribe, whom Moses had sent out to make preparations for entering from the wilderness of Paran (Num 13:1–3), to the south of the Land, produce a report that prompts the people to react with "Would that we had died in the land of Egypt! Or would that we had died in this wilderness! Why is YHWH bringing us into this land to fall by the sword . . . ? Would it not be better for us to go back to Egypt?" (Num 14:2–4). In response to Moses's intercession YHWH relents to let the exodus continue, but with a new generation. Those who saw the signs of YHWH in Egypt and in the wilderness will not see the Land but will die in the wilderness in accord with their own words. The journey will now take forty years (Num 14:20–24). The two spies who presented a good report, Caleb and Joshua, will be the two sole witnesses of the whole exodus as far as the entry into the Land (Deut 1:34–40); Joshua as the man from the Northern Kingdom of Israel (Josh 24:29–30) and Caleb for Judah in the south (Josh 14:6–15). In the composition of the book of Numbers we then also find the list of the old generation at the beginning (Num 2) and the whole of the other list of the new generation at the end (Num 26). The separation between the two is set in Deuteronomy 2:13–15 at the crossing of the Wadi Zered. It is this new generation that Moses addresses in the last book of the Torah. It is an example of the preaching that is always oriented to the future. YHWH:

> He established a decree in Jacob,
> and appointed a law in Israel,
> which he commanded our ancestors
> to teach to their children;
> that the next generation might know them,
> the children yet unborn,
> and rise up and tell them to their children,
> so that they should set their hope in God,
> and not forget the works of God,
> but keep his commandments;
> and that they should not be like their ancestors,
> a stubborn and rebellious generation,
> a generation whose heart was not steadfast,
> whose spirit was not faithful to God. (Ps 78:5–8)

Sabbath by Sabbath, each new generation must listen to the reading of the Torah. The whole of the book of Deuteronomy thus gains the character of a call to turn around, also in the sense of return from exile. The new generation is in the book before Moses, but the author has Moses take account also of the coming generations. The covenant is concluded anew in the time of the story in the land of Moab, at the last stopping place before the crossing of the Jordan (Deut 29:1), but YHWH speaks by the mouth of Moses, "I am making this covenant . . . not only with you . . . but also with those who are not here with us today" (Deut 29:13). The returning exile of all times may recognize himself in that nonpresent person as one who, listening to the book, is indeed there and belongs to the new generation. Although the old generation died in the wilderness—or in exile—as a result of its rebellion against YHWH, still the new one may identify with the old in relation to the covenant, to the giving of the Torah on Sinai. In the introduction to the Ten Commandments Moses therefore says very aptly, "YHWH our God made a covenant with us at Horeb. Not with our ancestors did YHWH make this covenant, but with us, who are all of us here alive today" (Deut 5:2–3). It is Moses who leads the people as far as the crossing of the Jordan, thus linking the old generation with the new. His words will indeed be heard by each new generation, until beyond the *exile.* That is the current situation, presupposed already in the book: if the people do not hear, they will be snatched out of the Land and be flung toward another land "as is now the case" (Deut 29:28). But if one lets these words *enter into* one's heart, during the exile, "If you *return to* YHWH your God . . . YHWH your God will bring about the great *turnaround* for you and *have compassion on* you, *turning* and gathering you from all the peoples among whom YHWH your God has scattered you. . . . YHWH your God will bring you into the Land" (Deut 30:1–4). The key moment of *return* from exile in the Prophets thus resounds already in the concluding phase of the exodus in the Torah.

5
"I Will Lead You into Exile"

In the Former Prophets the *exodus* reaches its goal. The people of Israel cross the Jordan with Joshua to receive the good, God-given Land. By means of the book of Judges the reader is taken to the "middle" of the Former Prophets, the *kingship* of David—and the building of the *temple* (2 Sam 7)—and in the books of Kings the reader witnesses the downward course of Israel's history, which ends in the exile.

The exodus from Egypt is mirrored in the entry into the Land: celebration of Passover (Exod 12)—on dry land through the Reed Sea (Exod 14)—wilderness—on dry land across the Jordan (Josh 3–4)—celebration of Passover (Josh 5:10–12). We have to wait to the end of the Former Prophets until we hear of a Passover celebration again: "The king [Josiah] commanded all the people, 'Keep the Passover to YHWH your God as prescribed in this book of the covenant.' No such Passover had been kept since the days of the judges [after Joshua] who judged Israel, even during all the days of the kings of Israel and of the kings of Judah; but in the eighteenth year of King Josiah this Passover was kept to YHWH in Jerusalem" (2 Kgs 23:21–23). Despite these good kings, despite this celebration around the temple, the exile is still going to take place. YHWH says, "I will remove Judah also from my sight, as I have removed Israel [cf. 2 Kgs 17]; and I will reject this city that I have chosen,

Jerusalem, and the house of which I said, 'My name shall be there'" (2 Kgs 23:27). The beginning is thus mirrored in the end: entry—Passover—events in the Land—Passover—departure into exile. Moses's book of the Torah also, with which Joshua entered the Land contemplatively (Josh 1:8–9; cf. Ps 1), has disappeared in the Former Prophets, until at the end it is rediscovered in the temple under King Josiah (2 Kgs 22). The books of Joshua to Kings are thus framed, in hope, by Torah and Passover. The author of the last chapters, however, offers no prospect of a return from the exile. For this we have to read the Latter Prophets. Here we are told only what we find already in the Torah, that if the Land is defiled, it will "vomit out" its inhabitants (Lev 18:25; 20:22): "So Judah went into exile out of its Land" (2 Kgs 25:21). The only indication that this does not mean the end of everything is a report on King Jehoiachin, who had already been transported off at an earlier date (2 Kgs 24:8–17). He is pardoned by Evil-Merodach, king of Babylon (2 Kgs 25:27–30).

1. "There Is No Knowledge of God in the Land"

The reason why YHWH says, "I will lead you into exile" (Amos 5:27) is enlarged upon by the prophets, Ezekiel in particular. Hosea puts it in a nutshell:

> Hear the word of YHWH, children of Israel,
> for YHWH has an indictment against the inhabitants of the Land.
> There is no faithfulness or loyalty,
> and no knowledge of God in the Land.
> Swearing, lying, murder, stealing and adultery have spread out,
> bloodshed follows bloodshed.
> Therefore the Land mourns,
> and all who live in it languish;
> together with the wild animals
> and the birds of the air,
> even the fish of the sea are perishing. (Hos 4:1–3)

It is also possible to read *earth* for *land* and thus create a link with the creation account: Israel as the representative of humanity among the land animals, the birds, and the fishes (cf. Gen 1:28). One of the many midrashic applications of the first sentence of this story, "In the beginning God created . . . ," reads: "With the Torah in mind—and the observance of Torah—God created heaven and earth." This application by the rabbis is appropriate from a biblical-theological perspective, as this passage from Hosea testifies. Where the Torah is no longer observed and so not really heard, the creation starts to refuse service. Moving out of Egypt on the pathway of the Ten Commandments, an echo of which can be heard in this text, is observance from which knowledge of God is born (cf. chapter 3, section 4). The same echo can be discerned in Jeremiah's temple preaching. The people think they are suitably pious with the threefold call "This is the temple of YHWH," but Jeremiah confronts this head on: knowledge of God means following the way of the commandments.

> If you truly amend your ways and your doings
> If you do not oppress the alien, the orphan, and the widow,
> or shed innocent blood in this place,
> and if you do not go after other gods to your own hurt,
> then I will let you dwell in this place,
> in the Land that I gave to your ancestors . . .
> What?
> Steal, murder, commit adultery,
> swear falsely. . . .
> I will cast you out of my sight
> just as I cast out all your kinsfolk,
> all the offspring of Ephraim [northern Israel]. (Jer 7:1–15)

In a vision Jeremiah sees what this means:

> I looked on the earth (the Land)
> and lo, it was waste and void;
> and to the heavens,
> and they had no light.
> I looked on the mountains
> and lo, they were quaking
> and all the hills moved to and fro.

> I looked
> and lo, there was no one at all,
> and all the birds of the air had fled.
> I looked
> and lo, the fruitful land was a desert,
> and all its cities were laid in ruins
> before YHWH, before his fierce anger. (Jer 4:23–26)

The creation has lost its objective; the departure from Egypt might just as well not have happened (cf. Judg 19:30). The whole of Jeremiah's prophecy resonates with this. YHWH speaks:

> I remember the devotion of your youth,
> your love as a bride,
> how you followed me in the wilderness. . . .
> What wrong did your ancestors find in me
> that they went far from me,
> and went after worthless things,
> and became worthless themselves?
> They did not say,
> "Where is YHWH,
> who caused us to go up from the land of Egypt?"
> (Jer 2:2, 5–6)

Nothingness, worthlessness, vapor. The word translated *worthless* here is a wordplay with "Ba'al," that is, with other gods.

> You came there
> and you defiled the Land,
> and made my heritage an abomination.
> The priests did not say, "Where is YHWH?"
> The Torah experts did not know me,
> the shepherds [of the people] rebelled against me,
> the prophets prophesied by Ba'al (Jer 2:2–8).

The question of the divine Name and what it means has fallen silent; knowledge of God in practice has been lost. It is the summary of what Jeremiah will subsequently cry in all sorts of tones and emphases, just like the other prophets, so that nothing else remains to prophesy than the central word of Amos: "I will lead you into exile" (Amos 5:27).

2. "Our Hope Has Flown Away"

The exile means the end of Israel. The Israelite people is submerged into the mass of nations, where, in deuteronomic terminology, they "will serve other gods" (Deut 28:64). There is no longer any difference in their creedal cry, "Hear O Israel, YHWH is our God, YHWH alone" (Deut 6:4). So has the event of "I am YHWH-your-God who caused you to move out of the land of Egypt, out of the house of servitude" proved to be a mere incident, a misadventure? Or does something else need to be told of the divine Name, something that in the final analysis is crucially important?

In the exile we hear the people calling, "My way is hidden before YHWH" (Isa 40:27), or Zion saying, "YHWH has forsaken me and my Lord has forgotten me" (Isa 49:14). The entire "Book of Comfort," Deutero-Isaiah (Isa 40–55), is an answer to this. Ezekiel, the prophet par excellence in the exile, signals that the whole "house of Israel" is saying, "Our bones are dried out, our hope has flown away, cut off—that is us!" (Ezek 37:11). The lifeline has been severed. The first expression that is used shows up when one recalls that a human being is "flesh and bones." The "weak" flesh is supported by the bones. You're in real trouble if you have to say, "My bones are out of joint" (Ps 6:2). If the bone marrow dries out (Ps 32:3), you are close to death. The expression "our bones are dried out," a way of expressing despair which sounds a little odd to modern readers, becomes in Ezekiel the germ of the vision that expresses the essential content of his preaching. The house of Israel has been scattered in the land of exile, the great valley of the Fertile Crescent, the land of the Two Rivers. He has to address his own people as individuals, soul by soul (Ezek 3:16–21). The community of people has been dashed apart, and he suddenly sees them before him in an image all too real for a person in antiquity. That is how Herodotus saw the sites where a battle had previously taken place: a valley of bones of the unburied fallen. "Our bones are dried out." The whole exile is a valley of dry, dead bones. Can these bones, these killed people (Ezek 37:3, 9), live again? Impossible! But when YHWH asks his prophet this, he answers, "You know." And then Ezekiel's whole ministry is summarized in the commission: "Prophesy over these bones and tell them [just as he had to say to the individuals of the people]: 'You dry bones, hear the word of YHWH'" (Ezek 37:4). The events are subsequently described very graphically, the climax being that the spirit is summoned from all four spirit/wind directions: "Blow into these killed ones, that they may revive. . . . And they stood on their feet, an army, very, very great" (Ezek 37:9–10). That's also how it was for Ezekiel himself at his call: "As soon as he spoke to me, the spirit came into me and made me stand on my feet" (Ezek 2:2) to exercise the prophetic ministry, to make the house of Israel stand on its feet, ready for their march of return from exile: a miracle beyond all miracles, like a resurrection from the dead. "Thus says my lord YHWH: see, I open your graves and will cause you to come out of your graves, my people, and bring you to the Land of Israel" (Ezek 37:12).

In the conclusion to the main part of the book of Ezekiel, we read the summary:

> Therefore, thus says my Lord YHWH,
> "Now I will bring about a turnaround for Jacob,
> and have mercy on the whole house of Israel
> and will be jealous for my holy name."

Despite their unfaithfulness they will again live safely in the Land. Thus YHWH proves himself as the Holy One in the sight of the peoples.

> Then they shall know
> that I am YHWH-their-God
> —when I let them go into exile among the nations,
> and then gathered them into their own land.
> I will leave none of them behind.
> I will never again hide my face from them,
> when I pour out my spirit upon the house of Israel
> —the word of God from my Lord YHWH. (Ezek 39:25–29)

In an unexpected and inconceivable manner the Name "happens" in this great return. The word *have mercy*, so typical of the unpacking of the Name in the Latter Prophets, occurs only here in the book of Ezekiel. This is similar to the way it sounded in the passage about the return in Deuteronomy 30:3.

3. Solidarity and Faithfulness

Two pairs of words in biblical language characterize effective, well-focused behavior. From the point of view of time, this is *solidarity* (NRSV and other versions: "steadfast love," "love," "loving-kindness") and *faithfulness*, and from the point of view of space, *righteousness* and *justice*. *Righteousness* indicates what someone is, *justice* what someone does. The good king in particular is said to be "upright" or "just" in doing just things (e.g., Ps 72:1–2), to those in "distress," such as the poor, orphans, widows, or strangers. In doing justly the upright person brings *space* for anyone in dire straits; he comes as a deliverer.

In the word pair in which the temporal aspect is determinative, the word *chesed*, which is difficult to translate (something like "loving-kindness/solidarity"), indicates what one does, and *faithfulness* indicates what one is. Faithfulness has to prove itself time and time again, in a reciprocal relationship, in a bond between you—my neighbor, my fellow—and me. You do me a deed of solidarity as a sign of faithfulness at a crucial moment when I most need it, and I do the same for you. For example, I meet you on my path and we decide to continue our walk together as travelling companions, fellows, as "neighbors" to each other. If I injure my foot along the way I can count on you to help me, to show *chesed*, solidarity toward me; and I do the same for you. If you don't do that and leave me incapacitated, then it's all over between us—our relationship, the bond between us, is broken. In fact, if you walk the same path that I was walking along and you find me by the wayside, then as "companion on the way" you become my "neighbor" and you won't pass by on the other side. YHWH has thus become Israel's ally in solidarity and faithfulness, and he expects that Israelites will follow his lead, both with respect to each other and to him. Solidarity works both ways.

That's how things are to be on YHWH's model farm with Ephraim (northern Israel) and Judah, who together are Jacob/ Israel:

> Ephraim was a trained heifer
> that loved to thresh.
> I placed a yoke on her fair neck:
> I will harness Ephraim,
> Judah must plough;
> Jacob must harrow for himself.
> Sow for yourselves righteousness;
> reap with an eye to *solidarity*,
> break up your fallow ground;
> for it is time to seek YHWH
> that he may come
> and rain righteousness upon you!
> You have ploughed wickedness,
> you have reaped injustice,
> you have eaten the fruit of lies. (Hos 10:11–13)

In Hosea 4:1–3 we find the word pair in full: "There is no faithfulness or solidarity, there is no knowledge of God in the Land" (Hos 4:1). The model farm has turned into its opposite. If solidarity is not consistently practiced by both parties, then it's all over! "I will not love you any more," says YHWH (Hos 9:15), but at the end of the book of Hosea we find the surprising statement: "I will love them freely, for my anger has turned from them" (Hos 14:4). What has happened in the meantime? What was YHWH's concern? "For I desire solidarity and not sacrifice; the knowledge of God rather than burnt-offerings" (Hos 6:6). But this knowledge is continually absent (Hos 4:6; 5:4; 6:3, 6; 7:9). They do call, "My God, we [Israel] know you!" (Hos 8:2), but it is not "with their heart" (Hos 7:14). They do not really hear what is being said to them: "I have been YHWH-your-God ever since the land of Egypt; you know no God but me, and besides me there is no savior. It was I who fed you in the wilderness" (Hos 13:4–5). How frustrating for him to have to say:

> What shall I do with you, O Ephraim?
> What shall I do with you, O Judah?

> Your solidarity is like a morning mist,
> like the dew that goes away early. (Hos 6:4)

The consequence is that they themselves will become "like the morning mist, or like the dew that goes away early" (Hos 13:3). If there is no reciprocity in solidarity, another interaction occurs. If Israel forgets YHWH, YHWH will forget Israel (Hos 4:6; 8:12–13). He found them as young grapes in the wilderness (Hos 9:10), and now Ephraim will dry out in the desert wind (Hos 13:15). It is said of Ephraim: "Out of Egypt I called my son" (Hos 11:1), but now, "to Egypt he shall return: Assyria will be his king" (Hos 11:5; 8:13).

Will Ephraim perish in exile? Will this be a catastrophe, a "turning upside-down" as of Admah and Zeboiim (and Sodom and Gomorrah, cf. Deut 29:23)? No, something else is "upside-down," namely the heart of YHWH. From the innermost core of his being, YHWH cannot give up on his son Ephraim:

> My heart turns around within me;
> all that is compassion in me grows warm,
> I will not act according to my fierce anger.
> I will not destroy Ephraim further,
> for I am God and no mortal. (Hos 11:8–9)

Strange, isn't it, that last sentence? So don't gods wreak punitive vengeance when their commands are disobeyed? But what is YHWH's command? That emerges from the fact that he can continue with his solidarity *unilaterally*. He does that by trickery, as it were.

His wife Israel, who has run after other gods, her lovers, has everything taken away from her (Hos 2:1–12). In fact it's even worse:

> Therefore I will now lead her astray
> and make her go into the wilderness. (Hos 2:14)

Life is impossible in the wilderness. She has to get out of the Land (Hos 9:3), and where does she end up? In exile! Ezekiel makes this metaphor explicit by speaking of "the wilderness of the peoples" (Ezek 20:35), but as a result of the story of the exodus the word *wilderness* also has a positive meaning. In the wilderness (*midbar*) the word (*dabar*) could be heard. Like someone in love, YHWH goes further: "And speak to her heart" (cf. Isa 40:2). For Jeremiah the wilderness period was the time of the bride (Jer 2:2) and that now becomes the time of the exile too:

> as in the days of her youth
> as on the day when she went out from the land of Egypt.
> (Hos 2:15)

When YHWH thus reveals his faithfulness from one side, continuing his solidarity unilaterally, what words would make this clear? The lover speaks:

> I will take you for my wife for ever;
> I will take you for my wife
> in righteousness and in justice,
> in solidarity and in *mercy*.
> I will take you for my wife
> in faithfulness,
> and you shall know me. (Hos 2:19–20)

The latter clause is daringly erotic but demonstrates that the solidarity will once again be mutual. *Faithfulness*, the dominant word, must be evident in the act of solidarity. Love cannot come from just one side. If, astonishingly, wondrously, that is indeed possible for YHWH, the solidarity is in fact mercy, and the people—"Lo-Ruchama" (one who receives no mercy)—may be called "Ruchama" (one who has received mercy). In the introduction to the dramatic second chapter, we read (in anticipation of the conclusion to the book, Hos 14:2–19) that the whole people *assembles* under the name "Children of the Living God." This is a term for the return from exile (cf. Jer 23:3). Judah and (northern) Israel meet again, as if this were a new exodus from Egypt. "They go up out of the land" (Gen 50:24; Exod 1:10) "under one head." A new Moses as a new David (cf. Ezek 37:15–28)? They greet each other and call to the brothers, "Ammi!" ("My people!"), and to the sisters, "Ruchama!" ("*Mercy!*"). That word loses its vague generality and gains color and meaning in the manifestation of the Name in the return from exile.

4. YHWH Turns Around to Zion

The word *rachamim*, "mercifulness/mercy"—and this also applies to the verb—does not occur exclusively in connection with the return from exile but often, and in a penetrating manner. If Isaiah 13 speaks of the demise of Babylon, the continuing text reads: "But YHWH will have compassion on Jacob and will again choose Israel, and will set them in their own land" (Isa 14:1).

In the Book of Comfort, Deutero-Isaiah, YHWH appears as the merciful one who prepares the way back from exile (Isa 49:10, 13).

> For a brief moment I abandoned you,
> but with great compassion I will gather you.
> In overflowing wrath for a moment I hid my face from
>   you,
> but with everlasting solidarity I will have compassion on
>   you. . . .
> For the mountains may depart and the hills be removed,
> but my solidarity shall not depart from you,
> and my covenant of peace shall not be removed,
> says YHWH, who has compassion on you. (Isa 54:7–10)

In the closing chapter of the Book of Comfort (Isa 55), like a trader at a market, YHWH offers his wares "free, for nothing," calling out, "Come, buy wine and milk, without money and without price," calling customers one by one, so that together they once again become his people, whom he can address in the plural:

> Seek YHWH while he may be found,
> call upon him while he is near;
> let the wicked forsake their way,
> and the unrighteous their plans;
> let them return to YHWH,
> that he may have mercy on them;
> to our God,
> for he will abundantly pardon. (Isa 55:6–7)

And so, in his mercy, the plans and ways of YHWH embrace—in the literary form too—those of his people:

> For: *my plans*
> are not your plans

and your ways
are not *my ways*. (Isa 55:8)

YHWH takes the resistance of his people so that he can move them again to return, so that he can remain the God-of-Israel. He will succeed in doing this. The superiority of heaven over the earth is the guarantee of this.

For: as the heavens are higher than the earth
so are my ways higher than your ways,
my plans higher than your plans.
For: as the rain or the snow
come down from heaven
and do not return there
until they have watered the earth,
making it bring forth and sprout,
giving seed to the sower,
and bread to the eater,
so shall my word be
that goes out of my mouth;
it shall not return to me empty,
but it shall accomplish that which was my will
and succeed in the thing for which I sent it. (Isa 55:9–11)

Because of fructification from heaven, the dry earth has a future (cf. Isa 45:8). With the recurrence of the word of mercy, Israel will have successfully reverted to being YHWH's people, turning again with him to Zion (Isa 40:10–11). When the walls are rebuilt as a sign of the return (Mic 7:11), on that day the way in which YHWH is "God" is revealed. As if in a wordplay on the name of the prophet of the book of Micah—"Who is like (YHWH)"—the conclusion of the book reads:

Who is a God like you,
pardoning iniquity,
and passing over the transgression
of the remnant of his inheritance [people]?
He does not retain his anger for ever,
but takes delight in solidarity;
who again has mercy on us. (Mic 7:18–19)

We read the same thing in the Psalms (e.g., Pss 102:14; 106:46). In Isaiah it is emphasized that first and foremost it is YHWH himself who returns (Isa 40) to accept the kingship in Zion and so make his name known (Isa 52:6–10). Similarly, according to Zechariah, YHWH says, "I have returned to Zion and live within Jerusalem" (Zech 8:3), and it is then that the community is there too: old men and women who sit, stick in hand because of their age, on the squares of Jerusalem—squares full of boys and girls at play. Return from exile? It is YHWH himself who returns first; the initiative for this event lies squarely with him: "I have returned to Jerusalem in mercy" (Zech 1:16; cf. 7:9; 10:6).

In unforgettable words, Jeremiah expresses how that initiative comes about, how mercy is an unimagined and unexpected, deep emotion that YHWH notes in himself. The concern in this case is first and foremost with Ephraim (northern Israel), YHWH's first-born son (Jer 31:9) who perishes in exile. Rachel, the matriarch, weeps for her children, refusing to be comforted for this lost son (31:15; cf. Jacob weeping over Joseph in Gen 37:35). In the exile Jeremiah cries out with a penitential bowing motion (as orthodox Jews do today at the Wailing Wall). YHWH is disturbed by this shouting and speaks in an inner monologue, full of amazement at himself:

> Is Ephraim such a dear son to me
> or a darling child?
> Yes, as often as I speak against him,
> I must really remember him!
> Therefore my insides are moved;
> I must have mercy, have mercy on him. (Jer 31:20)

My word *insides* is rather a flat translation. The prophet himself is said to be moved by the fate of his people. Using the same word he cries out with pain: "Woe, woe! My insides, my insides!" (Jer 4:19). We say something similar but more prosaic: "It's giving me stomachache!" The intestines are the physical site of the profoundest emotions. YHWH discovers, as it were, a hidden layer in his being which moves him now to demonstrate the most profound aspect of his Name: mercy. In the final analysis this is the crucial word. Despite having resolved not to have mercy (Jer 13:14), he has to give way to the inner compulsion (cf. Jer 12:15; 30:18; 33:26).

The following text describes the return to Zion:

> Set up orientation stones for yourself,
> make yourself signposts,
> direct your heart on the highway,
> the path that you take.
> Return,
> Miss Israel,
> return
> to those cities of yours. (Jer 31:21)

"Orientation stones" (NRSV, "road markers") is the translation of *ṣiyyun* (found elsewhere only in 2 Kgs 23:17 and Ezek 39:15). It's a play on words: these stones, as it were, bear the inscription "This way to Zion."

> Return,
> Miss Israel,
> return. . . .
> How long will you waver,
> you faithless daughter?
> Yes, Yhwh has created a new thing on the earth:
> female will encompass male. (Jer 31:21–22)

The last sentence is a notorious point of discussion. The neatest and most apt interpretation runs as follows: The invitation to return to the Land is presented as a prophetic "invitation to the dance." After all, how is the girl called to her dance in Song of Songs 6:13?

> Return, return, O Shulammite!
> Return, return, that we may look upon you.

The turns in the dance are adapted in Jeremiah to the turn toward Zion, but the invited girl, Israel, constantly averts her gaze, hesitating. She needs something out of the ordinary to persuade her. Usually it is the male partner who dances around the female. But on the way to Jerusalem the girl Israel will dance around her male partner, Yhwh. And that is how Yhwh returns with her to Zion.

6
"He Cannot Deny Himself"

The experience of emancipation took shape in Israel in the story of the exodus from Egypt. It is difficult to say when this happened. Anyone reading the story will notice right away that the speaker is not a historian but "Moses." We may assume that the five books were given shape in the Second Temple period and for all sorts of reasons conclude that the story itself is not historical. Of much greater importance is the conclusion that it expresses Israel's confession: We have become the people of YHWH by moving out and—as we celebrate Passover—repeatedly moving out from "Egypt," the house of slavery. We confess YHWH, who says, "I am YHWH your God who caused you to move out of the land of Egypt to be their slaves no more; I have broken the bars of your yoke and made you walk erect" (Lev 26:13). What is said here about the exodus can be read in almost the very same words about the exile and about the yoke that Nebuchadnezzar places upon the people (Jer 27): "On that day, says YHWH of hosts, I will break the yoke from off your neck, and I will burst your bonds. Strangers shall no longer make a servant of him [the people]" (Jer 30:8). This event does indeed have historical roots in the Babylonian captivity, which came to an end in the Persian period. But this does not tell the whole story; and not just because many remained behind in the land of captivity, so that exile became a permanent phenomenon in the history of the people, but primarily because the "historical" captivity became a "theological" theme, perhaps the most important theme for the understanding of TNK (Diebner).[1] Exodus and return from exile can be sung about in a single psalm:

> Hallelujah!
> O give thanks to YHWH, for he is good,
> for his solidarity endures for ever!
> Who can express the mighty doings of YHWH
> or declare all his praise? (Ps 106:1–2)

So begins the last psalm of the fourth collection. There is a subsequent reminder of the miracles of the exodus, of the liberation at the Reed Sea despite the opposition to YHWH and of the many events of the time in the wilderness; but also of the disobedience in the Land and the many rescues by YHWH. The conclusion of the song speaks of the exile:

> He regarded their distress.
> When he heard their cry,
> for their sake he remembered his covenant,
> and had compassion according to his great solidarity.
> He caused them to be pitied
> by all who held them captive.
>
> Save us, YHWH our God,
> gather us from among the nations,
> that we may give thanks to your holy Name
> and glory in your praise. (Ps 106:43–47)

If the miracles of YHWH at the exodus and his mercy in the return from exile, the two points of focus of TNK, are the two ways of telling of the Name, it is to be expected (1) that at the return, the exodus will play a part as the primordial beginning and as background in the Latter Prophets; but equally (2) that mercy should occur already in the Torah as the deepest mystery of the Name.

1 Editors' note: Bernd J. Diebner (1939–2023).

1. Exodus in the Prophets, Exile in the Torah

In the previous chapter it was already pointed out that in the book of Jeremiah the whole prophecy is marked by the exodus.

The prophet begins with the word of YHWH: "I remember . . . your love as a bride, how you followed me in the wilderness" (Jer 2:1). After their arrival in the Land, however, the people no longer asked, "Where is YHWH, who caused us to go up out of the land of Egypt?" (Jer 2:6).

Again and again there is a reminder of that beginning (Jer 7:22; 11:4; 32:21; 34:13), just like in the book of Hosea, so closely related in its bridal theme (e.g., Hos 11:1; 12:14; 13:4; cf. Amos 2:10; 3:1; 9:7; Mic 6:4; Zech 10:11, etc.); though there with the distinction that the return from exile is described in exodus terms. In *that* "wilderness" Israel once again becomes the bride (Hos 2:13–20). After the exodus and the time in the wilderness have been enlarged upon in Ezekiel 20, the exile is called "the wilderness of the peoples" and the return can be expressed in these words: "I will cause you to move out from the peoples and gather you out of the countries where you are scattered, with a mighty hand and an outstretched arm" (Ezek 20:34). The reader is familiar with the last clause from the Torah; the exodus took place "with a mighty hand and an outstretched arm" (Deut 4:34; cf. Exod 5:24; 6:5). My teacher, M. A. Beek, used to comment that Exodus 1–14 can be read as the Passover Haggadah of recurring exiles. In (Deutero-)Isaiah there are frequent reminiscences of the history of the exodus. YHWH's royal pathway with his people goes back to Jerusalem via the wilderness (Isa 40:3) but in a new way: "Do not remember the former things . . . ," says YHWH, "I am about to do a new thing . . . I will make a way in the wilderness and rivers in the desert" (Isa 43:18). The new exodus from Babylon is a new creation by YHWH, who earlier "made a way through the sea" and "destroyed horse and chariot" (Isa 43:16–17).

The mighty arm of YHWH is invoked to perform a deed as before:

> Was it not you who dried up the sea,
> the waters of the great deep;
> who made the depths of the sea a way
> for the redeemed to cross over?
> So the ransomed of YHWH shall return
> and come to Zion with singing. (Isa 51:10–11)

It is a surprising new exodus:

> For you shall go out in joy,
> and be led back in peace,
> the mountains and the hills before you shall burst into song,
> and all the trees of the field shall clap their hands (Isa 55:12).

Just as, in the Prophets, the exodus is not only the background to the return but also the model for it, so in the Torah the exile is already looming on the horizon, while the return is already in view as well. We met all this in the book of Deuteronomy. If Israel does not *hear*, it will be "cast away to another land" (Deut 29:28); if, when there, it allows the words of the Torah to sink in, it will turn around and return to the Land through the mercy of YHWH (Deut 30:1–10). In the book of Leviticus the detailed commandments are concluded with a chapter on blessing and curse. At the beginning of this chapter we again read, for reinforcement: "You shall make for yourselves no idols and erect no carved images . . . to worship at them, for I am YHWH your God" (Lev 26:1). Observance of the commandments will mean peace, but if not, then it will eventually lead to exile, to a scattering among the peoples (Lev 26:33). Even in the land of their enemies YHWH will not abandon them, however: "I will remember in their favor the covenant with their ancestors whom I caused to move out from Egypt in the sight of the nations, to be their God: I *YHWH*" (Lev 26:45). Even then—and especially then—his Name is at stake. The extent to which exile is the theological theme is given special weight in the introductory chapters of Genesis. Not only the story of the days of creation leading to the Sabbath but also the series of stories about the *condition humaine* (Gen 2:3–4:26) form the fundamental introduction to the beginning of the book proper. Positive and negative views of human being provide a background for "the book of begettings" (Gen 5:1). The man and his wife are driven out of the garden when they eat of the tree of knowledge of good and evil, that is, when they break the relationship with YHWH God. One might think of this as the first and great commandment. Man, as Cain, is driven from his field when he does not tolerate his brother next to him and murders him. One might think of this as the second commandment, equal to the first. Humanity wandering and roaming about on earth to the east of Eden (Gen 4:14, 16), without prospect in exile? The last sentence of this series of stories reads: "At that time people began to invoke the name of YHWH" (Gen 4:26). In the book of Jeremiah, which begins so forcefully with the exodus and ends just as forcefully with the exile in Babylon and in Egypt, the two themes come together in one pronouncement. The prophet speaks of the coming days, of exile in the "North," in Babylon, from where YHWH, as a shepherd, brings his flock back to the Land:

> The days are surely coming—says YHWH—
> when it shall no longer be said,
> "As YHWH lives
> who caused the children of Israel to go up
> out of the land of Egypt!"
> but
> "As YHWH lives who caused the offspring of the house of Israel to go up,
> and come out of the land of the north"
> and out of all the lands where he had driven them
> so that they should live on their own Land. (Jer 23:7–8; cf. 16:14–15)

Decisive though the second one is, it can only be said on the basis of the first, taking that as its model.

2. Abraham and Jacob

The exodus from Egypt and the return from Babylon, as the two focal points of TNK, as the two ways of telling about the divine Name, also define who Israel is. These two aspects must therefore be present in the book of the beginnings of Israel, in Genesis: in Abraham, Isaac, and Jacob. Isaac plays an intermediate part. He is the son of *father* Abraham and he is the father of his *son* Jacob. So then, Abraham is characterized by his exodus and Jacob by his return.

Abraham's "going" is a movement out of the land of the Two Rivers to the Land of Canaan: "Go from your country and your kindred and your father's house to the Land that I will show you" (Gen 12:1). That going of Abraham is performed in contrast to that of his father, Terah. When the (apparently) oldest son of Terah has died in Haran, "in the land of his birth, in Ur of the Chaldeans" (Gen 11:28), Terah takes Abram, Lot, and Sarai with him. And so it was that Abram and his people "went out together—Terah and his household—from Ur of the Chaldeans to go into the Land of Canaan. They came to Haran and settled there" (Gen 11:31), as if the narrator wants to say that there was nothing really special about this. They were content in Haran in the northwest of Mesopotamia. So why go on farther to Canaan? In the meantime Abram's exodus from the southeast of the Land, from Ur of the Chaldeans, has already begun. It seems as if YHWH has already started his plan with Abram without him being aware of it. Abram's going to Canaan is certainly brought to a good end, on the basis of his call. Abram took his people with him, and "they moved out to go to the Land of Canaan and they came to the Land of Canaan" (Gen 12:5). Having taken a detour to Egypt because of famine in Canaan, Abram has his exodus imposed upon him there by Pharaoh (Gen 12:10–20).

When the second half of the Abraham cycle begins and YHWH promises him a son, YHWH says, "I am YHWH, who caused you to move out from Ur of the Chaldeans, to give you this land to possess" (Gen 15:7). No reader will miss the parallel with the wording in the central books of the Torah, but will certainly find it rather surprising: the Chaldeans—surely these are the (Neo-)Babylonians of Nebuchadnezzar? Isn't that the people that is responsible for the exile (cf. 2 Kgs 25; Isa 43:14; Jer 21:4)? It seems as if the narrator drops these words so that the returning exile can identify with Abram: "Move out from Babylon, free from Chaldea!" (Isa 48:20).

Nonetheless it is the exodus from Egypt that Abram's descendants are characterized by, in this same chapter: they are to be servants to the Egyptians—the name is deliberately avoided—but "they shall move out with great possessions" (Gen 15:14).

Abram moves out, away from the land of his "begetting," to Canaan. For Jacob, Canaan is the land of origin, which he must leave because of his unbrotherliness. The movement he makes, however, is an about-turn. At Laban's in the land of the Two Rivers he is given the commission by YHWH: "Turn around, return to your country, to the land of your begetting" (Gen 31:13; cf. 31:3; 32:9). The quotation comes from the chapter in which Jacob and all that is his stand on the threshold of the Land. All he has to do is cross over the Jabbok. But will his return also be his turnaround? In his poem "Over de Jabbok," the Dutch poet Gerrit Achterberg writes: "When I had reached the end / of my corruptions / God stood up out of the mire / and wept."[2] Jacob can only cross the Jabbok, facing his brother and brotherliness, if the Name comes about over him and he accepts the name Israel—which occurs here for the first time in the Bible. How does the unnamed Name come about? "He blessed him there" (Gen 32:29). And what is its content, other than "YHWH is with you"? It is this Name that makes Jacob Israel. This turnaround characterizes Israel, and that is why they are present in the text, for the first time in the Bible: "the children of Israel" (Gen 32:32).

3. Twice the Name in Exodus

Ezekiel, the prophet who elaborates more than any other on the remorse of the people, the horrors of the devastation of Jerusalem, and the descent into exile, is the same Ezekiel who emphasizes more than anyone that YHWH acts for the sake of his Name.

2 Editors' note: Gerrit Achterberg, *Verzamelde Gedichten* (Amsterdam: Athenaeum-Polak & Van Gennep, 1991), 245.

We select as an example the chapter in which he brings exodus and exile together.

When elders of the people want to consult YHWH through the prophet, they are given the answer: "Say to them, 'Thus says my Lord YHWH: On the day that I chose Israel . . . making myself known to them in the land of Egypt . . . I am YHWH your God. On that day I swore to them that I would cause them to move out of the land of Egypt into a land that I had searched out for them, a land flowing with milk and honey; it is a jewel above all lands'" (Ezek 20:3–6). That Land can be called the Garden of Eden (Ezek 36:35; cf. Gen 3 and 4). But did YHWH stop the exodus from taking place because they had already fallen into idolatry in Egypt? No: "But I acted for the sake of my Name, that it should not be profaned in the sight of the nations among whom they lived, in whose sight I made myself known to them in causing them to move out of the land of Egypt" (Ezek 20:9). That's how things went time and again in the wilderness too, and subsequently in the Land, and the exile was the consequence, "the wilderness of the peoples." Now, however, YHWH will make his Name definitively known, after the model of what happened in Egypt: "And you shall know that I am YHWH" (Ezek 20:38). This refrain rings out time and again in the book. "On my holy mountain . . . there they shall *serve* me. . . . When I cause you to move out from the peoples. . . . And you shall know that I am YHWH when I deal with you for my Name's sake, not according to your evil ways" (Ezek 20:40–44). To characterize this act, Ezekiel uses once in his summary, as we have seen, the word *mercy* (Ezek 39:25).

In Hosea we came across the strange word combination *loving-kindness/solidarity* and *mercifulness* (Hos 2:19). If the mutual solidarity is absent, if the people's *chesed* has dispersed like a morning mist, YHWH continues, unilaterally, to maintain his *chesed*, his solidarity, as mercy. In relation to this unusual word combination, however, many think first of Psalm 103, so often used in liturgy. Anyone who blesses YHWH with his "soul," with "all that is within" him ("all that is within me bless his holy Name"), does it with the words "Who forgives all your iniquity . . .

who crowns you with *chesed*, solidarity and mercy" (Ps 103:1–5). Is the composer thinking of Hosea? Perhaps, but in the following text he refers to another text. He makes a noticeable change, but to the point, in line with his opening, in the saying: "Gracious and merciful is YHWH, long-suffering and great in solidarity" (Joel 2:13; Jonah 4:2; Pss 86:15; 145:8; Neh 9:17). He exchanges the first words: "Merciful and gracious" (Ps 103:8). The phrase occurs like this one other time in TNK, and the poet refers to that passage with the preceding verse: "He made known his ways to Moses." This is quickly found in a concordance. After the story with the golden calf Moses is not easily satisfied in his discussion with YHWH. When YHWH has said to him, "Go, leave this place, you and the people you have caused to go up out of the land of Egypt. . . . I will send an angel before you" (Exod 33:1–2), Moses responds, "See, you have said to me, 'Cause this people to go up,' but you have not let me know whom you will send with me. Yet you have said, 'I know you by name, and you have also found favor in my sight.' Now if I have found favor in your sight, *show me your ways*, so that I may know you" (Exod 33:12–13). The play on the word *know* prepares the reader for the call:

> YHWH, YHWH, God,
> merciful and gracious
> long-suffering
> and great in solidarity and faithfulness. (Exod 34:6)

This is the saying that the psalmist is quoting—and this is the only other place with the same word order: such are the ways of YHWH, that is how his Name occurs, which is to be blessed.

To Moses's request, "Make your ways known to me," YHWH responds: "Should *my face* (i.e., I myself in my familiar presence) go with you to set your mind at rest?" (Exod 33:14). And Moses said, "If *your face* is not going with me, do not carry us up from here." Only thus can it be *known* that "I and *your* people" have found favor in your sight; only thus that we are set apart, "I and your people," from every people on the face of the earth (Exod 33:16). In Israel God's Name is universally at stake. In this connection we must not forget the story of Moses's call. YHWH had come down to cause his people to go up. This verticality was accomplished by the horizontal commission to Moses: Go, cause my people to move out! (Exod 3:8–10). That was how the Name came about: I will be there as I will be there (Exod 3:14).

In the idolatry with the golden calf the people had distanced themselves from YHWH in two regards. They had called to Aaron: "Make gods for us, who shall go before us," that is, in place of YHWH who caused us to go up. But what they say is: "For this Moses, the man who caused us to go up out of the land of Egypt, we do not know what has become of him"—there, up on that mountain, because Moses delayed "to come down" (Exod 32:1). YHWH then distances himself from his people and says to Moses on the mountain, "Go down at once! *Your people* whom you caused to go up out of the land of Egypt, have acted perversely" (Exod 32:7). And again after the annihilation of the "golden god": "The people that you, Moses, caused to *go up* out of the land of Egypt" (Exod 33:1). But the very Name YHWH consisted in this! It should not come as a surprise that at this very point the narrator comes back to the Name. The golden calf, as the summary of the idolatry, is projected back from the history in the Land (see, e.g., 1 Kgs 12:28; 2 Kgs 10:29; Hos 8:5). At the heart of the matter the idolatry was the break with YHWH that led to the exile. So this datum is given already in the Torah. The worship of the golden calf brings YHWH to say to Moses, "Now let me alone, so that my wrath may burn hot against them and I may consume them" (Exod 32:10; cf. Ezek 10:13). And so YHWH also says to Jeremiah, for example, "Do not pray for the welfare of this people. . . . By the sword, by famine, and by pestilence I consume them" (Jer 14:11–12; cf. 15:1). Then, however, the Name seems to have a deeper dimension.

In his conversation with YHWH, after the promise that, in his familiar attentiveness, YHWH's face will go with the people, Moses goes one step further: "Show me your glory, I pray" (Exod 33:18). Moses will indeed see this, if only in passing, but at the same time he will hear something essential. Moses will not see the face of YHWH, only his "back" when YHWH has gone past. But YHWH says:

I will make all my goodness
pass before your face.
I will proclaim
the Name YHWH
before your face:
that I am gracious to whom I will be gracious
and will show mercy on whom I will show mercy. (Exod 33:19)

In this the reader hears a surprising further explanation of the divine Name: I will be there, just as I will be there. Even after the people's break with YHWH through the episode with the golden calf, he will be there as the gracious and merciful one. But when this happens, the words swap places: merciful and gracious (Exod 34:6). Although in the Torah everything is about the exodus, in essence the theme of the Prophets is already there as well. The story of the one Name is told in two ways in the book of Exodus: the exodus from Egypt and YHWH's return to his people. The authors' presentation reflects the two ways in which YHWH himself originally makes his Name known—the second on the basis of the first, as the prophets can speak only of the return from exile in terms of the story of the exodus. Without having first heard of the emancipation from Egypt one cannot confess, with Psalm 103, "who has pardoned all your transgressions," as the latter are only given concrete shape on the basis of the Torah. "Sin" is in fact *forgetting* that you have moved out of Egypt, and "forgiveness" means that the deepest inner part (Jer 31:20) of the Name comes over you.

The writer of the Second Epistle to Timothy, "Paul," has the Torah and the Prophets in his mind when he writes of the Messiah, Jesus: "The saying is sure: If we have died with him, we will also live with him; if we endure, we will also reign with him; if we deny him, he will also deny us." But this is followed by the surprising lines, "if we are faithless, he remains faithful—for he cannot deny himself" (2 Tim 2:11–13). From the perspective of the TNK you could say: The divine Name occurs in Jesus.

4. "Who Has Shown Mercy to Him"

The words "merciful" (*rachum*) and "gracious" (*chanun*), both of which occur thirteen times in TNK, are used only of YHWH. It's the same with the word *eleos*, "mercy," in the Gospel of Luke, which occurs almost exclusively in the first chapter: in the songs of praise of Mary and Zechariah (Luke 1:46–55; 1:68–79), both of which are so imbued with the language and texts of the TNK. We come back to what was said above in chapter 1. Mary sings:

> My soul magnifies the Lord. . . .
> For the Mighty One has done great things for me. . . .
> And his mercy is from generation to generation. . . .
> He has helped his servant Israel,
> in remembrance of his mercy.

When the neighbors and relatives hear of the birth of Elizabeth's son, they rejoice because the Lord has shown great mercy to her (Luke 1:58), and Zechariah raises his prophetic song of praise:

> Blessed be the Lord God of Israel,
> for he has looked favorably on his people . . .
> to show mercy to our ancestors. . . .
> To give knowledge of salvation to his people
> by the forgiveness of their sins,
> by the inner [NRSV: "tender"] mercy of our God.

From the texts Luke is alluding to, it is clear that in the Greek Bible which he is consulting, both "solidarity" (*chesed*) and "mercy" are rendered by *eleos*. But in Luke it is exclusively used in relation to the Lord, the God of Israel. This has to be borne in mind if one wants to understand what he means when he uses it one more time in his Gospel (Luke 10:25–27).

A Torah scholar tries to test Jesus, with the question: "Teacher, what must I do to inherit eternal life, true life?" But you are a Torah scholar yourself, aren't you, sir? So the person being tested is not tricked into providing an answer and replies, "What is written in the Torah? What do you read there?" Well, as a Torah scholar he is able to put it succinctly and well: The first and great commandment and the second one like it, You shall love the Lord your God with all your heart . . . and your neighbor as yourself; as you are, that is how he is too. The conversation can then be brought quickly to a conclusion with Jesus's words: "Do this, and you will live." You can imagine that the Torah scholar feels a bit cheated. He wants to justify himself. The two commandments, that's easy to say, but it's right there that the problems start. "And who is my neighbor?" That's odd! He skips the first commandment and doesn't say "And who is God?" In Luke's Hellenistic world the answer to that question is far from clear. But isn't it necessary even in the world of Scripture readers to provide fresh answers to the question of who and how is the Lord your God? Is Luke going to leave that question to one side when he puts a parable on Jesus's lips?

Someone goes down from Jerusalem to Jericho (why take that route?) and falls into the hands of robbers. He lies along the wayside, cleaned out and injured. We note the reversal that is already hinted at here. Not "Who is my neighbor, so that I can do something for him in love?" but "When you're lying completely helpless, half dead, on the side of the road, will a neighbor be there for you?" A priest comes down along the way, from *Jerusalem*. What has he been doing in Jerusalem? He will have just had his finest hour, his turn as priest, just like Zechariah (Luke 1:8) in the temple service—the liturgical form of loving God. And now he stands before the second commandment on this pathway and passes by on the other side. *Likewise*, a Levite, also from the temple, where he has been following the priest step by step with his Levitical service. And here again, he passes by on the other side. But a Samaritan, on a journey . . . a merchant, or something like that. If by some chance he was coming from Jerusalem, then that wouldn't be from the temple, because that's not where Samaritans practice the liturgical celebration of the first commandment. It is precisely for that reason that this third passerby in the parable has to be a Samaritan; they worship God on Mount Gerizim near Shechem (cf. John 4:20). The Samaritan isn't meditating on a temple service he has just witnessed; he is simply on a journey. But when he sees the victim of a robbery lying there, he is moved with compassion and sees to everything that needs to be done, touchingly and efficiently. Suddenly the parable is over and Jesus now poses the question to his conversation partner: "Which of these three, do you think, was a neighbor to the man who fell into the hands of robbers?" The answer is simple: the third one, the Samaritan. But why this reversal, then? The Torah scholar's question was "Who is my neighbor?," and he is forced to identify himself with the person lying beaten up by the wayside. With his surprising answer Luke makes it clear that the man gets the point: "The one who showed him mercy." Isn't that at the same time the answer to the silent question, "Who is God?" Luke used that little word *mercy* only in the first chapter and exclusively for the God of Israel, who has turned to his people "to show mercy" (Luke 1:72).

One small thing remains unclear, however. Why did the Levite need to appear in the story? "*Likewise* a Levite"; both in the temple and along the pathway he was entirely the follower of the priest. Now if the Samaritan is referring to God, who has shown mercy, the question arises: Should the God of Israel also have a follower? The Torah scholar is told: "Go and do *likewise*" (Luke 10:37). In the letter to the Ephesians, the community is comforted and admonished like this: "Therefore be followers of God, as beloved children, and live in love, as Christ loved us" (Eph 5:1). Isn't that what the prophet Zechariah also means when he says to his compatriots, using that strange word combination (Hos 2:18; Ps 103:4), "Thus says YHWH of hosts: Render true judgments, show solidarity and mercy to one another" (Zech 7:9)?

What can you say about "God," apart from the dual narrative exposition of the divine Name in Moses and the Prophets? What is left is not much more than some form of *deism*—in the *Oxford English Dictionary* definition, "belief in the existence of a God, with rejection of revelation." Achterberg chose that word as the title of a poem, the heart of which is an allusion to the parable of the Good Samaritan. It is as if the speaker is the man who fell into the hands of robbers, who clean him out and leave him lying by the wayside.

Man is for a time a place of God.
If no equals sign still holds him firm,
then he is transcribed on a stone.
The agreement seems to run to
this completion, this abrupt end.

For God goes further, wheeling off from him
in his millions. God is never alone.
For the former it would be the turn of another.

We are for him a full petrol tub
which he leaves empty. He must be rid of it,
all the rubbish, at odds with his being.

Since he differs from the creation
we would fall dead and lie beside the path,

if Christ, merchant in scrap iron,
had not had to find us just in such a condition;
as if he had been whispering with the Father.[3]

[3] Editors' note: Achterberg, *Verzamelde Gedichten*, 932.

7
The Song of Praise and the Songs of Ascent

If the theme of "exodus and the return from exile" defines the Torah and the Latter Prophets so prominently, it would be strange if the Writings, the third category of TNK, did not bear traces of it as well. When thinking of the second focus point, for instance, the exile, who would not be reminded of the book of Lamentations, read in the synagogue on the day of mourning, Tish B'Av, the Ninth of Av, in early August, the day of commemoration of the destruction of the temple?

> How lonely sits the city
> that once was full of people!
> How like a widow she has become,
> she that was great among the nations!
> She that was a princess among the provinces
> has become a vassal.
>
> She weeps bitterly in the night,
> with tears on her cheeks;
> among all her lovers
> she has no one to comfort her;
> all her friends have dealt treacherously with her,
> they have become her enemies. (Lam 1:1–2)

It is because of the exile (Lam 1:3) that Jerusalem, daughter Zion, is in such a state. Her deported population is groaning in search of bread, as *goyim*, forbidden to enter, have penetrated into the sanctuary (Lam 1:10). Her lot is bitter (Lam 1:4), because there is no one to revive her spirit (Lam 1:16, 19). Nonetheless, the lament can turn around into hope:

> It is through the works of solidarity of YHWH,
> that we are not cut off,
> his mercies never come to an end.
> They are new every morning;
> great is your faithfulness. (Lam 3:21–22; cf. 3:32)

That is why Lamentations ends with the prayer:

> Restore us, YHWH, to yourself,
> that we may be restored;
> renew our days as of old. (Lam 5:21)

Lamentations—at the Ninth of Av—is one of the five feast scrolls, like the Song of Songs at Passover, Ruth at Shavuot (Pentecost), Ecclesiastes at the Feast of Tabernacles, and Esther at Purim. In the little book of Ruth there are perceptible echoes of Lamentations. Naomi, the main character, appears there like the figure sung about in a Yiddish song:

> *In dem beys-hamikdosh*
> *in a vinkl-kheyder*
> *sitzt di almone bas-Tsion aleyn.*

In a quiet corner of the sanctuary sits the poor widow, daughter Zion, lonely and alone, as in Lamentations 1:1. Naomi returns from exile as a widow without children (cf. Isa 54:1) wanting to be called Mara, "bitter" (Ruth 1:5, 20; cf. Lam 1:4), in Bethlehem, the "House of Bread," where YHWH gives bread again (Ruth 1:6; cf. Lam 1:11). Her return succeeds because Ruth, the Moabite woman, from a people that was not allowed to enter into the community of YHWH (Deut 23:1; cf. Lam 1:10), bears a son for her who brings back her spirit (Ruth 4:15–17; cf. Lam 1:16, 19).

The feast scroll Song of Songs, read at Passover, does not speak of the exodus, but one can still hear the love songs as an answer, for example, to Jeremiah's characterization of the exodus as the days of a bride (Jer 2:2). The book of Esther plays out in the exile, where we meet Mordecai as the descendant of a Benjaminite who was deported with the exiles (Esth 2:6; cf. Dan 1:1–4). On the other hand the book of Ezra–Nehemiah, which follows the conclusion of Chronicles, tells of the return (2 Chr 36:22–23; Ezra 1:1–4).

In the first book of the Writings, the Psalms, we meet the exodus, of course, in the epic songs (such as Pss 78, 105, 106, 136), but also as reference to the beginning of the covenant (e.g., Pss 74:2; 81:6, 11). The most famous psalm about the exile is Psalm 137: "By the rivers of Babylon, there we sat down, there we wept as we remembered Zion" (Ps 137:1). Many psalms of lament can be imagined in the exilic situation. Sometimes this is also made explicit. The figure who prays, "Save me, O God, for the waters have come up to my neck [my soul]. . . . Answer me, YHWH, for your solidarity is good; turn to me, according to your abundant mercy" (Ps 69:1, 16), ends his prayer with "For God will save Zion and rebuild the cities of Judah and his servants shall live there" (Ps 69:35). And so Psalm 79 begins with the destruction of temple and city. The prayer for reconciliation culminates in "Then we your people, the flock of your pasture, will give thanks to you for ever; from generation to generation we will recount your praise" (Ps 79:13).

Two series of psalms deserve special attention: the so-called Hallel (Pss 113–118), which is associated with celebration of Passover, and the Songs of Ascent (Ha-ma'alot, Pss 120–134), in which the ascent from exile is celebrated in song.

1. "Why Is It, O Sea, That You Flee?"

From ancient times, the psalms of the Hallel have formed a liturgical series. They are sung by the Jewish family in the household's celebration each year on the eve of Seder. Jesus did this too, during the Passover meal with his disciples: they sang the Hallel, the song of praise (Matt 26:30; Mark 14:26). It is a celebration of the time "when Israel went out from Egypt" (Ps 114:1), but the preceding Psalm 113 also tells us who the Israel of the exodus is, as Genesis does in the Torah. Israel is what it is by virtue of the Name. In the first strophe of Psalm 113, with three lines of seven words, we hear the call to praise the Name in the fullness of time, "From this time on and for evermore"—and in geographical terms, "from the rising of the sun to its setting." In the middle strophe the Name is expounded in seventeen words—the numerical value of YHWH.

> YHWH is high above all nations,
> and his glory above the heavens.
> Who is like YHWH our God,
> who is seated on high,
> who looks far down
> on the heavens and the earth? (Ps 113:4–6)

The movement is in an upward direction: above the earth—for good reason described here as "above all nations," *goyim*—even above heaven, in fact. There he has his *seat* and his *view*. The assonance of the Hebrew words for *high* and *low* brings this out to some extent. By this means the poet achieves a special effect. He does not say, "Who is like YHWH in heaven and on earth?" (cf. Deut 3:24; 2 Chr 6:14), but as he has spoken of the glory of YHWH *above* heaven, the view is now in a downward direction: He *looks* into heaven and upon the earth. But in the depths, on earth, he reveals his unique *elevation* by *elevating* the poor:

> He raises the poor from the dust,
> and lifts the needy from the ash heap,
> to make them sit with princes,
> with the princes of his people;
> he gives the barren woman a home,
> making her the joyous mother of children. (Ps 113:7–9)

YHWH is *seated* so high so as to give that man and that woman their full place so that they can be *seated*; a patriarch and an infertile matriarch (the association with Sarah is unmistakable for any reader of the Bible) may sit—with princes? Yes, but with princes of his *people* and in the *house*. The people and house of Israel, that is what this man and this woman represent! The downward-directed elevation of YHWH "above the *goyim*, the nations" is revealed in the elevation, in the midst of the *goyim* (v. 4), of Israel, which "went out from Egypt, the house of Jacob" (Ps 114:1). This first song of the Hallel is framed by "HalleluYaH!"

The twelve words of the first strophe of Psalm 114 summarize the whole exodus from Egypt to the promised Land:

> When Israel moved out from Egypt,
> the house of Jacob from a people of strange language,
> Judah became his sanctuary,
> Israel his dominion. (Ps 114:1–2)

Whose sanctuary? Certainly, with the conclusion of the Reed Sea song it's easy to give the answer: "You brought them in and planted them on the mountain of your own possession, the place, YHWH, that you made your abode, the sanctuary, YHWH, that your hands have established" (Exod 15:17). But in this psalm the answer is reserved for the last strophe. The one who stands for what this song sings of is Jacob's God, the "master of the whole earth" (Ps 114:7). When the people cross the Jordan and enter the Land, "the ark . . . of the lord and master of the whole earth" passes before them (Josh 3:11, 13). The poet evidently has this story from Joshua in mind, because besides the sea (the Reed Sea) which they cross with dry feet, he also has the Jordan appear, which people cross on dry land (cf. Josh 4:23, 24)—both personified.

> The sea looked and fled;
> Jordan turned back.
> The mountains skipped like rams,
> the hills like lambs. (Ps 114:3–4)

Once again the psalmist summarizes the entire history of exit and entry in twelve words. The whole earth reacts with horror: in its stable form of mountains and hills, and in its unstable form of sea and river. These are what we call natural phenomena, but in TNK they frequently stand as metaphors for historical factors. The sea can mean the sea of the nations (e.g., Isa 17:12–18; Rev 17:15), which threatens Israel. The river can represent the one threatening power that is in a position to sweep Zion away (e.g., Isa 8:7;

Ps 124:4–5; Rev 12:15). The mountains can be a metaphor for the great kingdoms and thus the hills for the smaller ones. Psalm 46 brings this out strikingly in the comparison: mountains shake, waters roar and foam (vv. 2–3), nations/*goyim* are in uproar, kingdoms totter (v. 7).

The geographical data of the stories in Exodus and Joshua thus gain added current value. The hilarious way in which they are brought up—who has ever seen the sea fleeing or a river doing an about-turn?—also reminds us that in its history Israel has had to contend with the swamping sea of the peoples. Israel experienced the irresistible power of a kingdom like a mountain (cf., e.g., Matt 17:20), to their cost. Even when they enter the Land under Joshua, there are kingdoms there, large and small. "Joshua took all these kings and their land at one time, because YHWH, the God of Israel, fought for Israel" (Josh 10:42). The "mountains" and the "hills" leaped away in fright. But how does the psalmist arrive at "mountains . . . like *rams*" (Ps 114:4)? They may come from a passage in the Reed Sea song, to which he will soon make a further allusion.

> The peoples heard, they trembled,
> *cowering* gripped the inhabitants of Philistia.
> Then the chiefs of Edom were dismayed,
> trembling seized the *rams* of Moab. (Exod 15:14)

The word *rams* is not usually translated literally but rendered by "leaders" (cf. NRSV). But precisely this special Hebrew term must have been the source of inspiration for Psalm 114. The whole earth—all its inhabitants included—reacted with horror and flight at the exodus (so too at the crossing of the Jordan in Josh 5:1; cf. the allusions there to Exod 15:14, 16).

Is this psalm a historical song? In any case it's a liturgical song too. At the Passover meal, one has to participate as if one is leaving Egypt oneself. It is happening now, so in the third strophe (of two times seven words) the singer speaks of the "earth" in the present tense: "Why is it, O sea, that you flee?" After that a great silence descends, as it were, as sea and Jordan, mountains and hills do not answer.

Who YHWH is and what he does cannot be discerned from nature or the world of peoples, but only from the story of exit and entry that Israel itself tells. But the special event of the twelve tribes has general, universal significance. The singer addresses the earth universally—once again with two times seven words—and authoritatively, with an allusion to Exodus 15:14:

> Before the face of the (Lord and) Master,
> *cower* O earth,
> before the face of Jacob's God,
> who turns the rock into a pool of water,
> the granite into a spring of water. (Ps 114:7–8)

The Lord and Master of the whole earth (Josh 3:13; cf. Zech 4:14) is Jacob's God. What is typical of him? He turns rock into water. Does the poet mean by this only the scene in the wilderness in which water comes out of the rock (Exod 17:6)? No—judging by the last parallel line he must have Deuteronomy 8:15 in mind: YHWH "led you through the wilderness . . . an arid waste-land; he made water flow for you from that *granite rock*." The last double word gave him the parallelism with which he concludes his song, and in the same, bold way in which he spoke of the sea, the Jordan, and mountains. To paraphrase: Where it is as dead as a rock, as infertile as hard granite, he brings about the transformation to water of life. Twice at the end of the lines he ceremoniously drops the word *water* and so he expands the image: it is Jacob's God who gives life in the midst of death. Isn't this the central theme of the Passover? On the eve of Seder people recite: "With our forefathers God also redeemed us. . . . It is therefore our duty to thank, laud, praise, honor, exalt, glorify, bless, raise up, and extol him who . . . caused us to move out of servitude to freedom, from pain to joy, from mourning to celebration, from darkness to the great light, from slavery to the great redemption." And so the rock turns to water. Psalm 114 is a song with hilarious features, which is sung joyfully, because it is about the celebration of the exodus.

The following psalms have no direct connection with the exodus. Psalm 115 can be taken as a song for along the way—for instance in Joshua 24:23: "Put away the foreign gods and incline your hearts to YHWH, to YHWH, the God of Israel." "*Not to us*, YHWH, not to us, but to your name give glory, for the sake of your solidarity and faithfulness" (Ps 115:1). "May everyone who makes idols be as dead as his creations clearly are" (Ps 115:4–8). "The gods do not praise YaH . . . *but we*, we bless YaH, from this time on and for evermore" (Ps 115:17, 18). Israel does not own its God and cannot display him in an image—a golden calf—but in blessing YHWH, this people is blessed (Ps 115:12–15).

In Psalm 116, anyone joining in with the singer arrives, freed from "the bonds of death," in "the courts of the house of YHWH" and says with the last words in direct speech and as a greeting, "in your midst, *Jerusalem*." This place is, after all, the goal of the Passover story. There all the *goyim* are called upon to praise YHWH (Psalm 117). Finally the unexpected, delivered deliverer comes into the gates in procession and is received as a priest. "Blessed is he who comes in the name of YHWH" (Ps 118:26). We know the messianic interpretation and application from the Gospels (Matt 21:9; Luke 19:38; John 12:13). We know that this psalm was partly responsible for shaping the church liturgy (Hosanna, Benedictus), but we must not overlook the fact that this song is the conclusion to the Hallel. As the Reed Sea song of Moses is expressly quoted: "YaH is my strength and my might; he has become my salvation" (Ps 118:14); similarly in the directed prayer: "You have become my salvation" (Ps 118:21); "You are my God, and I will extol you" (Ps 118:28). The unnamed figure sings, repeating Moses's words:

> YaH is my strength and my might,
> and he has become my salvation.
> This is my God,
> and I will praise him,
> my father's God [cf. Exod 3:6],
> and I will exalt him [Exod 15:2].

The Hallel *is* the exodus story, sung about time and time again, each time afresh: "I shall not die, but I shall live," which means "and recount the deeds of YaH" (Ps 118:17).

2. "Like Watercourses in the Negev"

In the book of Chronicles, Solomon speaks the following words in his temple consecration prayer: "If they sin against you . . . and you give them to an enemy, so that they are carried away captive to a land far or near . . . then if they repent with all their heart and soul in the land of their captivity, to which they were taken captive, and pray towards their Land, which you gave to their ancestors, the city that you have chosen, and the house that I have built for your Name—then hear from heaven . . . maintain their cause and forgive your people who have sinned against you" (2 Chr 6:36–39). Here, in Solomon's last prayer, just as in 1 Kings 8:46–53, the coming exile is presupposed in veiled terms. In Kings we read the exodus addition, omitted here: "For they are your people and heritage, which you caused to move out of Egypt, from the midst of the iron-smelter" (1 Kgs 8:51). Here, at the end of the last book of the Former Prophets, there is no mention of the return from exile. But at the end of Chronicles there is—and the current rabbinic division makes it the conclusion of TNK. All the universality of King Koresh/Cyrus is directed to a particular project when he says, "YHWH, the God of heaven, has given me all the kingdoms of the earth, and he has charged me to build him a house at Jerusalem, which is in Judah. Whoever is among you of all his people, may YHWH his God be with him! Let him *go up*" (2 Chr 36:23).

In the Latter Prophets this word is most commonly used for the exodus, but also for the return from exile (e.g., Jer 16:14–15). In Ezra–Nehemiah the returning exiles are called "those who go up or have gone up" (Ezra 2:1, etc.). And the text there begins with a specifying quotation from 2 Chronicles 36:23 (Ezra 1:3, 5). There is a striking clause about Ezra, who begins "the *going-up* out of Babylon" to Jerusalem on the first day of the first month (Ezra 7:9). In the plural the word usually means "stairs" (e.g., Neh 12:37). The inscription above Psalms 120–134, Songs *ha-ma'alot*, can thus also be translated as "staircase-songs"—in accordance with tradition, because Levites sang these songs on the fifteen stairs at the Nicanor Gate of the temple. But generally speaking, translators opt for the meaning "go up to Jerusalem." This is what *Israel* does especially before the three great feasts (Deut 16:16; cf. Matt 20:17). That is why often the translation "pilgrimage songs" is preferred. Although that is not incorrect, strictly speaking only Psalm 122 is a pilgrimage song. The more accommodating meaning of Songs of Ascent offers the advantage that the association with going up out of exile is left open. At first sight there is only one psalm that has the return as its theme: Psalm 126. On closer inspection, the theme of "going-up" from a foreign country, from the existence of slavery, out of the forced labor to Zion, is discernible in three series of songs: one series of three and two of six songs. In the first series it is already apparent that the exile should be thought of not so much "historically" as thematically. On the first and certainly literal arrival in Jerusalem (Ps 122), for instance, Zion lies far from in ruins but accepts the accolade of being "built as a city that is bound firmly together"; but isn't any pilgrimage a going up from foreign parts to the House of YHWH, a memorial of the return from exile? The songs will certainly originate in the Second Temple period, a long time after the first exiles returned, as described in Ezra–Nehemiah, but the divine Name, "who caused Israel to go up out of the land of the north (Babylon) and out of all the lands where he had driven them" (Jer 16:15), becomes tangible *time and time again*, even for those who live in the Land. We have to bear in mind, by the way, that many of the people did not return, and that "exile," *galut*, in Babylon "and all the lands," has become a lasting phenomenon since the sixth century. In addition, the diaspora extended westward, in particular into Egypt. The wide "scattering" among the peoples is presupposed by many prophetic texts. In Isaiah 60 the coming of glory to Zion is coupled with the return of the sons and daughters who are pressed by peoples and kingdoms—in the opposite direction to the deportation into captivity. The "sea of peoples" comes there offering its gifts, from Midian to Kedar, from all ends of the earth (Isa 60:4–7; cf. Zechariah).

The first Song of Ascent can be taken figuratively as well as "literally." In the former case an individual speaks of his escape from a juridical situation, in which a false witness almost precipitated him into disaster. He characterizes the people, possibly his own compatriots in the Land, as peace haters. "Woe is me, that I am an alien in Meshech, that I must live among the tents of Kedar" (Ps 120:5). He feels like an exile. Or is he a figure from Israel in the diaspora, from Meshech on the Black Sea in the west to the nomadic lands of Kedar in the east? Wherever Israel is in foreign parts, it is threatened and persecuted as if in a falsely conducted legal trial: "*Rabat, long enough* my soul has lived there with peace-haters" (Ps 120:6), and so this psalm becomes a Song of Ascent, before on the way singing a "Song *for* the Ascent [Ps 121:1], to be sung to the Keeper of Israel, who guards the going out and coming in, exodus/departure and arrival" (Ps 121:8). When his feet have come to a stop in the gates, the returnee calls out, "Ask for the peace of Jerusalem" (Ps 122:6). In three psalms the ascent to Zion is accomplished.

Twice the same movement, each time with different accents, is repeated (Pss 123–128 and 129–134), beginning with the typical words: "*Rabat, enough*, our soul has more than had its fill of the scorn of those who are at ease" (Ps 123:4) and "*Rabat, enough* have they attacked me" (Ps 129:1); the two series end with "YHWH bless you from Zion" (Pss 128:5; 134:3).

Psalm 123 depicts the situation of male and female slaves in exile. One can imagine them standing ready behind their masters' and mistresses' tables. A mere wave of the hand and they immediately run at the master's or mistress's bidding. With no less tense attention, Israel watches the hand of YHWH but then "until he is gracious to us" (Ps 123:2), because our soul has had enough of this humiliation.

"If it had not been for YHWH who was on our side"—let Israel say in the following psalm—"then we would have been swallowed up alive" (Ps 124:1, 3). Waters would then have gone over our soul, but

> Blessed be YHWH,
> who has not given us as prey to their teeth.
> We have escaped like a bird

from the snare of the fowlers.
The snare is broken
and we have escaped.
Our help is in the Name of YHWH,
who made heaven and earth. (Ps 124:6–8)

In order to be such a help to them, he made heaven and earth. The universality is at the service of the special escape from the exile. And that means orientation toward Mount Zion, toward Jerusalem, even if it is still in the hands of foreign rulers (Ps 125:3, as in the historical time of the exile). The future will be "Peace upon Israel." When that happens, it's like a dream, but it is real. Psalm 126 sings of that moment.

The first verse of Psalm 126 presents difficulties, both grammatically and in view of corrected copyists' errors. Text and transmission may perhaps be taken into account like this:

If YHWH brought back those who were taken away . . .
we were like those who dream!
Then our mouth was filled with laughter,
and our tongue with shouts of joy;
then it was said among the nations:
YHWH has done great things for us
and we rejoiced!
Take us back, YHWH,
like the watercourses in the Negev. (Ps 126:1–4)

The first sentence can also be translated as "*When* YHWH brought back." Has it already happened, or is this expressing the hope of something that has not yet occurred? The ambiguity continues on in the subsequent text. The great return has been accomplished, but haven't "we" once again found ourselves in exile, having to pray, "Take us back"? Let us experience this, with vigor, like watercourses in the land of the south. This land of the south is deserving of its name: hot and dry, the Negev. The gullies and riverbeds lie without water. Only in the brief rainy season, when heavy showers pour down, the loamy ground crusts over, so that the water does not permeate it but seeks a path through the wadis, which suddenly and impressively become watercourses, wild torrents of water: water in the dry land. There could hardly be a more graphic image of the miracle of the return. What needs to happen between the "already" of verse 1 and the "not yet" of verse 4? Sow in order to reap. The suggestion has in fact been made that "shedding tears" in the sowing season is a rain rite; but if this is correct, then this is also a metaphor. In mourning and remorse they wait in the exile for the harvest of the future. "May those who sow in tears reap with shouts of joy" (Ps 126:5). Is it coincidental that the forty-eight words of the song form the numerical value of "Zion"? Be that as it may, the words in the exact middle are "YHWH has done great things for us, and we rejoiced." It is Labuschagne who draws our attention to such details.[1]

A key moment in the return is the rebuilding of the temple (see, e.g., Haggai). That aspect is given attention in Psalm 127. And the song itself is "of Solomon," the temple builder. But isn't the house that needs to be built just as much the House of Israel? "Unless YHWH builds the House, the 'builders' [*bonim*] labor in vain, because the inheritance for YHWH's sake are 'sons' [*banim*]. He provides for his *beloved* during sleep" (127:1–2). In the middle word of the psalm we hear an echo of the name of Solomon: Jedidiah, beloved of YHWH (cf. 2 Sam 12:25). Now, in the last psalm of this second series, the family of Israel can gather around the table in the middle (Ps 128:3): "May YHWH bless you from Zion," as we hear the definitive call, "Peace be upon Israel" (Ps 128:5–6).

It is enough. That is how the first song in third series begins as well, full of imagery of forced labor. The cords of the draught-animal are cut through (Ps 129:4), the people are free, and the Zion haters will miss out on the blessing of the harvest (Ps 129:8; cf. 126:6). What aspect has not yet sounded? That it is Israel's fault that it ended up in exile: "a song of ascent, out of the depths" (Ps 130:1). As part of the series it is not a psalm with a general awareness of sin but a song that puts into words the situation

[1] Editors' note: see, e.g., Casper J. Labuschagne, *Numerical Secrets of the Bible: Introduction to Biblical Arithmology* (Eugene: Wipf and Stock, 2016).

of alienation resulting from the break in the relationship with YHWH. The divine Name is hope and forgiveness: "Hope, O Israel, in YHWH" (Ps 130:7).

That sentence is repeated by the anonymous figure of Psalm 131, who has learned to stop raising his eyes with pride. He has managed to calm his furious soul. The image he uses becomes clear when one remembers that in antiquity the mother only stopped breastfeeding when her child was around three years old. A newly weaned toddler can whine, "Like a weaned child with its mother, like a weaned child, so is my soul within me" (Ps 131:2). "Of David," we read in the inscription. With this the little song moves over to the messiah in the exile of Psalm 132. He may be identified with the anointed one from the ending of Psalm 89, to which reference is made with words and expressions. "Remember what is my portion of life . . ." here in the exile, "where they taunt the footsteps of [me], your anointed" (Ps 89:47, 51). The end of the exile is marked not only by the reconstruction of the temple (Ps 127) but also by the rule of a "shoot of David" (e.g., Jer 33:15). And so I, your anointed in exile, call: "Remember, YHWH, in David's favor all the hardships he endured" (Ps 132:1), how he brought the ark to its resting place and how the public cult began in Zion (Ps 132:3–9; cf. 1 Sam 6). And so now: "For your servant David's sake do not turn away the face of [me], your anointed" (Ps 132:10). He then recalls the prophecy of Nathan (Ps 132:11–13; cf. 1 Sam 7). Surely sons, Davidides, should sit on the throne "for evermore!" YHWH's answer (Ps 132:14–18) is that he has chosen Zion as his dwelling place. The cult will flourish there again. There he will once again install the priests in their office. "There I will cause a horn [strength] to *sprout up* for David; I have prepared a lamp for my anointed one" (Ps 132:17). The crown which, according to Psalm 89:39, was "defiled in the dust," "will gleam on him" (Ps 132:18). And so the return from exile has the prospect: "The days are surely coming—says YHWH—when I will raise up for David a righteous Shoot, and he shall reign as king and deal wisely, and shall execute justice and righteousness in the land/on earth" (Jer 23:5; cf. Ezek 36:22–28).

In the Eighteen Benedictions the synagogue congregation prays:

> Turn back in mercy to Jerusalem, your city
> and dwell in her midst, as you have spoken
> and build her up. . . .
> The Shoot of David, your servant,
> make it quickly put forth shoots.
> May his horn rise through your salvation,
> for in your salvation we hope all day long.
> Blessed be you, YHWH,
> who makes the horn of salvation spring up.
> (Benedictions 14 and 15)

The prophetic words about the kingship in connection with the return to Zion are followed by a song on brotherhood, expressed in priestly imagery:

> How very good and pleasant it is
> when brothers live together in unity.
> It is like the precious oil on the head,
> running down upon the beard,
> on the beard of Aaron,
> running down over the collar of his robes.
> It is like the dew of Hermon,
> which falls on the mountains of Zion.
> For there YHWH ordains the blessing,
> life for evermore. (Ps 133)

Anyone speaking of biblical kingship is saying in the same breath: brotherhood. What brothers are meant in Psalm 133? The "hostile brothers" Jacob and Esau. A reference is being made to their blessing in Genesis 27:28–29, because that is the only place where olive oil and dew come together in a blessing (Hemelsoet). The return to Zion offers the prospect of brotherly reconciliation. Now Jacob and Esau, unlike in Genesis 36:7, can "live together." The anointed prophet does not have to prophesy against injustice between the brothers. The anointed king does not have to intervene to administer justice to the brother who is disadvantaged. This leaves the third anointed one, the (high) priest, but the poet sets him down at the moment of his anointing so as to depict the messianic secret of the brotherhood, in its full official form: Aaron, his head, his beard, the collar of his priestly vestments (Exod 28:32). He is the image of the reconciliation on Zion, toward which the exiles are on their way. There the priests will exercise their office before all the sisters and brothers, in the function they have been specially entrusted with—blessing (Pss 133:3; 134).

3. Blessing by the Blessed

In some translations the beginning of Psalm 134 reads, "Praise, o praise the Lord," or "Behold, praise the Lord." But this misses the heart of the song:

> Come, *bless* YHWH, all his servants,
> who stand in the House of YHWH by night!
> Lift up your hands in sanctification
> *and bless* YHWH!
>
> May YHWH bless you from Zion,
> he who made heaven and earth. (Ps 134:1–3)

When the Hebrew word was still translated with *benedicere*, "to pronounce a benediction," there was no difficulty. In many situations in our day (e.g., blessings by the pope, *urbi et orbi*), it is associated with making the sign of the cross. In Hebrew the term was used of man toward God. After the development of liturgical language in the past fifty years, no one will have a problem if the conclusion of Psalm 134 is translated "Blessed be YHWH from Zion." In Ephesians 1:3, where "bless" is the motif as in Psalm 134, the NRSV even begins with "Blessed be the God and Father of our Lord Jesus Christ, who has blessed us in Christ with every spiritual gift." Why is this important? Because blessing is a reciprocal act. In Psalm 129:7 this comes out splendidly in the failed harvest of the Zion haters. They cannot greet each other, as Boaz and his servants do at the harvest (Ruth 2:4), with the words

> The blessing of YHWH be with you,

to which the answer is

> We bless you with the name of YHWH.

To bless is to greet and so enter into fellowship with one another. One who blesses meets the one he greets with the commitment of his being: I am with you, in the expectation that you will be with me too. People bless each other to and fro, confirming that they will be there for each other, that they will let each other share in what they are and can do. That's how it is in the relation between YHWH and his people, too. They bless each other. So does YHWH need his people's blessing? Certainly, because he has invested everything he is and does in Israel and so for his people he wants to be the one blessed by Israel, so as to let them share in his blessing. *Blessing* is a word that characterizes the covenant relationship to such an extent that YHWH only wants to be the blessed one as the one blessed by his *human being*.

People bless each other with the Name of YHWH. That only makes the commitment greater. The blessing "YHWH be with you," *dominus vobiscum*, means "and I too, in following YHWH." When Jacob asks his enigmatic opponent at the Jabbok for his name, he is given the clear answer "Why do you ask me for my Name?" and in the same breath, "And he blessed him there" (Gen 32:29). That is, I am with you, because this is also the Name disclosed to Moses at his call (Exod 3:12). Conversely, Israel distinguishes itself from the peoples and their gods by saying "But we, we bless YHWH" (Ps 115:18; cf. vv. 12–15): we can't live any other way than in commitment to YHWH, our God.

Of the evangelists, it is Luke who gives special emphasis to mutual blessing. Zechariah the priest blesses the God of Israel (Luke 1:64, 68), as does Simeon in the temple (Luke 2:28), who also blesses Mary, Joseph, and the child. In the last account in his book, Luke ends with the blessing. Jesus blesses his disciples. "And it came to pass, while he was blessing them, that he withdrew from them. And they returned to Jerusalem with great joy [cf. Luke 2:10] and they were continually in the temple blessing God" (Luke 24:50–53).

In Psalm 134 the people call on the priests to bless YHWH, and they say to the people, "May YHWH bless you from Zion." On the ascent to the temple he will *keep/guard* you (Ps 121). He will let his familiar presence, his face light upon you and be *gracious* to you (Ps 123). He will lift up his countenance upon you and give you *peace* (Ps 125, 129). As the sun rises, so his face gives light (cf. Gen 32:30–31). As the sun climbs to its zenith, so he lifts his countenance to set his people in the full light of his day.

> YHWH spoke to Moses:
> "Speak to Aaron and his sons:
> Thus you shall bless the Israelites.
> You shall say to them:
> 'YHWH bless you and keep you.
> YHWH make his face to shine upon you
> and be gracious to you.
> YHWH lift up his countenance upon you
> and give you peace.'
> So they shall put my name on the children of Israel.
> I will bless them." (Num 6:22–27)

Jethro says at the exodus:

> Blessed be YHWH,
> who has delivered you from the hand of Egypt,
> from the hand of Pharaoh. (Exod 18:10)

The psalmist says at the return from the exile:

> Blessed be YHWH,
> who has not given us
> as prey to their teeth. (Ps 124:6)

The great blessing at the end of Book II of the Psalms reads:

> Blessed be YHWH God,
> the God of Israel,
> who alone does wondrous things.
> Blessed be the Name of his glory for ever.
> May his glory fill the whole earth;
> Amen and Amen. (Ps 72:18–19)

Epilogue

The dual theme of exodus and return is the theme of the Law and the Prophets. It scarcely appears at all explicitly in the letters of the apostles (cf., e.g., 1 Cor 5:6–8). This is not to say that the latter are not "structurally" "in accordance with the Scriptures" (1 Cor 15:3–4). Paul summarizes the atonement with a sharpening of the preaching of the prophets: "For God has imprisoned all in disobedience so that he may be merciful to all" (Rom 11:32). The evangelist Mark, however, writes his book about Jesus as a "Passover haggadah" (Hanhart).[1] Matthew underlines this, by making reference in his introduction to the exodus from Egypt (Matt 2:15). In the Gospel of Luke, Moses and Elijah speak with Jesus "of his exodus, which he was about to accomplish at Jerusalem" (Luke 9:31). "Before the festival of the Passover, when Jesus knew that his hour had come" (John 13:1).

And the return? This is included in the story as an appeal. Mark begins with a combination of quotations (Exod 23:30; Mal 3:1; Isa 40:3), "As it is written"; "See, I am sending my messenger/angel." In the framework of the Scriptures, the Law and the Prophets, Isaiah being mentioned by name, John the Baptist

[1] Editors' note: Karel Hanhart, *The Open Tomb: A New Approach, Mark's Passover Haggadah ([ca.] 72 C.E.)* (Collegeville: Liturgical Press, 1993).

appears, introducing the gospel: baptism with confession of sins. It is in this milieu that Mark has Jesus speak his first words: "The time is fulfilled, and the kingdom of God has come near. Repent, and believe in the gospel" (Mark 1:15). The name of Isaiah has been mentioned, and so the reader immediately thinks of the already cited Book of Comfort (Isa 40–55). That begins with the announcement of the return of YHWH, recognized by the "flock" of exiles he brings with him as the shepherd of his people (Isa 40:11). He comes to receive the kingship on Zion. This occurs in Isaiah 52:6–7, where YHWH once again makes his Name known by saying, "See, here I am." The joyful messenger then cries out to Zion: "Your God is king!" This does not mean the eternal kingship of YHWH but the event that is taking place at that moment: your God has taken upon himself the kingship (so also in Ps 93:1; 97:1). The hearer takes the proclamation as news. A new age has dawned. The messenger calls out the "gospel"—the word *good message* is borrowed from Isaiah 52:7—over Zion. The task given at the beginning, "Comfort, comfort my people" (Isa 40:1) is being fulfilled. People can observe the return of YHWH with their own eyes: "YHWH has comforted his people, he has redeemed Jerusalem" (Isa 52:9). There are already returnees. But where are the many who have remained in exile? The words of Isaiah 55:6–7 are addressed to them: "Seek YHWH now, while he may be found. Call upon him now, while he is near! Let the wicked forsake their way, and return to YHWH."

Jesus says, "The time is fulfilled. The *kingship* of YHWH has come *near*. *Turn around* and believe in the *gospel*" (Mark 1:15). It means just what Paul writes: "We entreat you on behalf of Christ, be reconciled to God. . . . See, now is the day of salvation" (2 Cor 5:20–6:2). Turn around to Zion, where the kingship of Israel's God has come near—only now in the crucified Messiah, while the temple is in ruins (Mark 13). "King and temple" will be the next topic (also the topic of a second book in this series). The John of the book of Revelation sees the lamb that was slain standing on Zion (Rev 14:1) and hears in the singing that YHWH God has received the kingdom (Rev 11:17). In the new great exile, too, everything remains oriented to Jerusalem, and the temple, though in ruins, remains, in the messianic era too, the place from where the Scriptures emanate.

The natural starting point for this first volume of a "concise biblical theology" lay in what the Apostolic Writings point to as the prime authority: Moses and the Prophets. We have taken this mainly in the narrower sense of Torah and Latter Prophets, though we have heard from the whole of TNK, the Psalter in particular (Luke 24:44): biblical theology following the canon of the ecclesia; in its reformed shape, since only the books of the Hebrew Bible were taken into account. This was done, moreover, correcting the customary sequence of the "Old Testament" and instead following the sequence of the three categories of the Hebrew Bible: TNK. Despite that connection with the synagogue, considerations remained within the time and space of the ecclesia, and not just because we always read the Apostolic Writings alongside them. No matter how much has to be learned there, the synagogue reads TNK differently. For the ecclesia "the days of the Messiah" have dawned, in which *goyim*, baptized in the name of Jesus, read with the synagogue from this perspective. In the words of the letter to the Ephesians, they may regard themselves as "fellow-citizens of the saints and members of the household of God" (Eph 2:19). As *fellow*-citizens—and only so—they may read the story of exodus and exile as their own as well, without for a moment losing sight of the fact that the words were spoken to Israel. They have a share in the blessing of Abraham. Israel, as the people of YHWH, remains for them the representative of humanity. A Jesus separated from Israel is no longer the Christ.

The church is accustomed to reflecting theologically upon preaching and pastoral care. How might you speak theologically about the two focal points of Torah and Prophets, which together form the single midpoint? That has to be done in what is classically the central part of a dogmatics: Creation—*Atonement*—Redemption, but on the basis of the biblical structure the part on the atonement can no longer—as was traditionally the case—begin with the *locus de peccato*, the doctrine of sin. How can one reflect on this without remembering the divine Name, beginning with the exodus and then also progressing resolutely with the return? *Dominus vobiscum*, "the Lord be with you," says the officiant in the worship liturgy. When Jacob asks at the Jabbok for the name of the person who has so mysteriously crossed his path, he is given an action as his answer: "And he blessed him there." YHWH is *with* you. His Name, his "being," is an action: God of Israel, God of his people, and so God *for* his people. The greatness of his glory consists in the fact that he wants to be the "small god of human beings" (Ad van Nieuwpoort), even against all resistance.[2] This heart of the matter is found in the beginning of the Gospel of Matthew, where on God's behalf it is said to Joseph, "She will bear a son and you shall call his name 'Jesus,'" but also, "And they shall call his name 'Immanuel'" (Matt 1:21–23). Jesus, "YHWH saves"; Immanuel, "God with us." The one name in a twofold manner: "He will deliver/save his people—and with Israel the *goyim*—from their sins," and that is how "*God with us*" takes place. That's why in theology—and in preaching—the first thing to speak of is not "sin" but the Name; how else would you know what the word *sin* means?

So where do we go from here? How do we know of the little word *God* from "God with us"? In Egyptian slavery it happened to "us" that we became emancipated. The one who caused us to move out: that's the one from now on we call "God." He has included us, Israel, in his covenant. Through Jesus the community had to face this. *Goyim* from afar have come up close. Jesus reveals precisely that the special covenant with Israel has been agreed for them too, and so the community is addressed first and foremost about grace, surprising and free. *This covenant is the presupposition of reconciliation.*

The prophets proclaim that YHWH maintains his covenant against resistance, against the sin of breaking the covenant by his people. Man does not want to live from grace, not realizing that only this would be life in freedom. He opts for other lords and

2 Editors' note: Ad van Nieuwpoort, *De kleine mensengod* (Amsterdam: Prometheus, 1996).

gods. Must Israel's God now remain simply God in the heights and not in the depths, above heaven and not on earth (Ps 113)? It is the "intermezzo" of "sin" that sets its face against the fulfillment of the covenant, hugely, in every regard. But if the word *omnipotence* is appropriate anywhere, then it is here. He is able to conquer the unfaithfulness of his human being through his faithfulness, whatever the cost. "Immanuel" is given shape in Jesus, who saves his people—and with Israel the *goyim*—from their sins. *Reconciliation is restoration of the broken covenant.*

The writer of these words is not a systematic theologian and would point out that others have written about reconciliation in this manner before[3]; but this book is written in the spirit of Abraham's words in Luke 16:31: "If they do not listen to Moses and the Prophets, neither will they be convinced even if someone rises from the dead."

3 Karl Barth, *Kirchliche Dogmatik* IV/1, 1–83.

Also in This Series

Divine Rejection: Explorations in the Biblical Portrayals of Esau and King Saul
R. J. Balfour